THE CHRISTIAN YEAR

THE CHRISTIAN YEAR

—

A GUIDE FOR WORSHIP AND PREACHING

—

ROBIN KNOWLES WALLACE

Abingdon Press
NASHVILLE

THE CHRISTIAN YEAR
A GUIDE FOR WORSHIP AND PREACHING

This book is printed on acid-free paper.

Library of Congress Cataloging-in-Publication Data

Wallace, Robin Knowles.
   The Christian year : a guide for worship and preaching / Robin Knowles Wallace.
      p.   cm.
   ISBN 978-1-4267-0300-3 (book - pbk./trade pbk., adhesive - perfect binding : alk. paper)
1. Church year.   2. Common lectionary (1992)   I. Title.
   BV30.W273 2011
   263'.9—dc22

2010048199

The names and dates of historical figures are in accordance with *The Oxford Dictionary of the Christian Church*, edited by F. L. Cross; 2nd revised edition edited by F. L. Cross and E. A. Livingstone (New York: Oxford University Press, 1990). Words in bold are defined in place. All website links were current as of September 2010.

11 12 13 14 15 16 17 18 19 20—10 9 8 7 6 5 4 3 2 1

MANUFACTURED IN THE UNITED STATES OF AMERICA

CONTENTS

ACKNOWLEDGMENTS

Thanks to Cordelia Burpee, Michele Lynne Holloway, and Robin D. Dillon, pastors all, for sharing their work. I also offer my thanks to the ecumenical body of liturgical scholars, whose research has informed this work, and to my husband, John, for traveling through the liturgical year with me year after year.

CHAPTER 1

THE CHRISTIAN YEAR IN BROAD STROKES

GOD'S TIME: KEEPING OUR PERSPECTIVE

For Christians, worship puts us into God's time—past, present, and future—in which, through the power of the Holy Spirit, we encounter Jesus Christ and learn to live in the present "between memory and hope" (phrase from Thomas J. Talley, "History and Eschatology in the Primitive Pascha," in *Between Memory and Hope* [BMH] [Collegeville, Minn.: Liturgical Press, 2000], 109). As we re-present the Christian story in worship each week, we hope for God's future that has been promised through scripture. Practicing the Christian or liturgical year proclaims the "acceptable year of our God," reminding us that it is God's vision and rule that are paramount, not human calendars. As the church moves through the spiral that is the Christian year, we celebrate promises made and kept by God and hopes given to us by the God of mercy, truth, justice, and love. We tell the story of the God of our weary years and silent tears, who has brought us through another day. We tell of creation, of flawed human beings who were called into greatness, and of ordinary people who under God's guidance became a holy nation, a royal priesthood.

Some theological-liturgical words that describe God's time:

Anamnesis (from Greek)—remembrance of the past that re-presents; for example, in remembering Jesus in communion we recognize his

1

presence with us now; in preaching the gospel we proclaim the reign of Christ not simply in the first century but also now.

Prolepsis (from Greek)—the breaking of God's future into the present day, "the kingdom of God is among you" (Luke 17:21b).

Presence—the ability given by God through the Holy Spirit so that we might experience God in the current moment that holds together past and future, living in the "already-not yet."

The Revised Common Lectionary (*RCL*), keyed to the liturgical year and developed by the Consultation on Common Texts (CCT) (http://www.com montexts.org/rcl/index.html), unifies denominations and congregations through a common pattern of biblical proclamation, incorporating a wide variety of scriptures. The North American ecumenical CCT adapted and revised the *Roman Catholic Lectionary for Mass*, 1969 (after Vatican II, 1962–1965); the *Common Lectionary* was approved on a trial basis in 1983 and the *RCL* was published in 1992. The *RCL* is used throughout this book.

HOW THE CHRISTIAN YEAR DEVELOPED

Robert F. Taft, S.J., reminds us that there is no ideal model of the Christian calendar, but that it is the task of each generation to build up the body of Christ for love and service of God and neighbor ("The Liturgical Year" in *BMH*, 23). The liturgical year is not described in scripture, but grew out of Jewish roots and was shaped by various political, psychological, theological, and geographical factors as the church developed.

Sunday

Each Sunday celebrates the mystery of creation, resurrection, and new life in the Spirit. Sunday has been called "the Lord's day," the day that belongs to God and over which God rules, and "the eighth day," the day of God's new creation (Epistle of Barnabas, Alexandria, written A.D. 70–

100). Each Sunday is the heart of the liturgical year, an opportunity to encounter the risen Christ in worship (Mark Searle, "Sunday: The Heart of the Liturgical Year," chapter 2 in *BMH*). To the Jewish concept of Sabbath (and ensuing issues of Saturday versus Sunday as Sabbath keeping), and the Christian emphasis on Sunday as the day of resurrection, Searle adds that Sunday is theologically and experientially a time of life after death: we have confronted Christ's death through our baptism and survived it to become people of the resurrection (69). Therefore, we no longer see people and creation through the lens of their usefulness to us, but through God's vision of their intrinsic worth. Therefore, we attend worship not because of duty or its merit for us, but because we are part of the body of Christ that is a joy and delight (see also the third-century Syrian Didascalia, translation found in Lucien Deiss, *Springtime of the Liturgy* [Collegeville, Minn.: Liturgical Press, 1979], 176–177).

The Beginning of Seasons and Holy Days
Other than Every Sunday

At the end of the third century, the Christian church had three primary holy days: Pascha, Pentecost, and Epiphany. By the end of the fourth century, each of these had separated into distinct days. Pascha, an ancient word that refers both to the passion of Christ and his passage from death to life at the resurrection (Patrick Regan, O.S.B., "The Three Days and the Forty Days" in *BMH*, 126), was separated into eight days of observances, including Palm Sunday, Holy Week, Holy or Maundy Thursday, Good Friday, Holy Saturday, and Easter Day. Pentecost separated into Ascension and Pentecost, on the fortieth and fiftieth days after Easter, respectively. Epiphany separated into Christmas (Dec. 25), Circumcision or Holy Name (Jan. 1), Epiphany (Jan. 6), and the Presentation of Christ in the Temple (Feb. 2) (James F. White, *Introduction to Christian Worship*, 3rd ed. [Nashville: Abingdon, 2000], 57, diagram 5).

The Paschal Cycle: Death and Resurrection

The Pascha, which evolved into Easter and Holy Week observances, began in the early church with commemoration of the passion and suffering of Jesus, the fast connected with the crucifixion and the time in the tomb, and observance through the night (Thomas J. Talley, "History and Eschatology in the Primitive Pascha" in *BMH*, 102). Remember that Sunday/Resurrection is the church's first celebration. Christians in Asia Minor and throughout the early church followed a practice, believed to reach back to the apostle John, of celebrating Easter on whatever day of the week worked in conjunction with the Jewish Passover on the Hebrew calendar dates beginning on Nisan 14, giving them the name **Quartodecimans**. The Quartodecimans celebrated a vigil, feasting and reading from the Hebrew Scriptures in the evening, and then after midnight proclaimed the resurrection of Jesus Christ and celebrated Eucharist, all a source of today's practice of the Easter Vigil. The Quartodecimans were the most important of the groups of people around controversies in the first millennium of the church for setting the date for Easter. Recent scholarship suggests that rather than being a deviation, the Quartodeciman practice was the original practice of the primitive community, after the weekly Sunday observance (Thomas J. Talley, "Liturgical Time in the Ancient Church" in *BMH*, 26). Therefore, the earliest festival we know of in the church is this unified celebration of Christ's death and resurrection at the Easter Vigil or Pascha.

Controversy still exists today about the date for Easter, because of different computations for setting the date for Easter between the Western (Roman Catholic and Protestant) and Eastern (Orthodox) churches. Augustine (354–430, bishop, northern Africa) lived during the time when the Pascha/Easter Vigil became multiple observances. His phrase for what we now call the Triduum (pronounced trĭ/-du-um) was "the three most holy days," the period from Holy Thursday evening, using the Hebrew accounting of "day" beginning with evening (cf. Gen. 1:5b), up to the evening of Easter. Thus the "three" are Good Friday, Holy Saturday, and Easter Sunday, with the evening of Holy/Maundy Thursday included. Patrick Regan suggests that this means that Easter, or the Pascha, begins with Thursday's communion service, that Good Friday has "as much to do with Jesus' glory as with his suffering," and that the Easter Vigil has as much to do with Jesus' death as with his resurrection (*BMH,* 139); in God's time in our worship we should seek to hold these tensions together as much as possible. Regan also notes that Easter, rather than simply being a co-opting of the name of the pagan goddess of the dawn Eostre, comes ultimately from the old Teutonic *auferstehung,* meaning "resurrection" (*BHM,* 134).

The Thursday of Holy Week has been celebrated since the early centuries of Christianity with commemoration of the Last Supper and celebration of the gift of communion, foot washing (John 13:3-17), remembrance of Jesus praying in the garden of Gethsemane, and a ritual known as **the stripping of the church** (removing all paraments and coverings or removing crosses and images) in preparation for Good Friday. It is foot washing that gives this day the title **"Maundy"** from the word *mandatum,* as Jesus gives the disciples a new mandate, or commandment, "that you love one another... as I have loved you" (John 13:34-35). Some traditions call this day **Holy Thursday** if they are not doing foot washing but only communion, and **Maundy Thursday** if they include foot washing and communion.

Good Friday draws its name from God's Friday or the Friday that became good for all humankind because of Jesus' work on the cross. Worship on this day focused on veneration of the cross, reading of the Passion from the Gospel of John, intercessory prayers, and the devotional practice of the Way of the Cross, often called Stations of the Cross. (**Devotional practices** can be done individually; the Way of the Cross will be discussed in chapter 5.) The works of Cyril of Jerusalem and the diary of Egeria (a Spanish nun who kept a meticulous record of her visit to the Holy Land at the end of the fourth century) recount that Good Friday in Jerusalem was spent venerating a relic of the cross at Golgotha during the morning, followed by a service of readings and hymns from noon until 3 P.M. The "Three Hours" service, which is common in many areas today, draws in part from this experience that was revived in the seventeenth century by priests in Peru, who based their service on the seven last words of Jesus from the cross. Laurence Hull Stookey (*Calendar: Christ's Time for the Church* [Nashville: Abingdon, 1996]) and others suggest that this multi-gospel approach takes away from the integrity of each gospel-teller, and they suggest instead the traditional reading of the passion story from the Gospel of John (see chapter 2 in this book for cautions about the passion story in John's Gospel). One tension regarding this practice for local churches may be the many cantatas arranged around the seven words. Better alternatives would be to intersperse the reading of a single gospel's passion story with hymns and spirituals about the cross from the perspective of that gospel.

Friday night into Saturday morning is the time that some traditions name as Jesus' descent to the dead in order that they might also know salvation, thus **Holy Saturday** is marked in the church by quiet and fasting. Some churches are open this day for prayer.

After the mid-fourth century in the West the **Easter Vigil** regularly included candidates who would be baptized or celebrate their first communion as the rooster crowed; there are references to baptisms on this day as early as the second century. The service itself was fourfold: the lighting of the Paschal candle, service of the Word, baptism, and communion; the Eastern Church followed the order of Word, light, baptism, and communion. Readings for the service of the Word varied throughout history; the oldest recording of readings at the Vigil is a fifth-century Armenian lectionary, where the first three readings are the creation story, the binding of Isaac, and the Passover narrative. Through the centuries, the Vigil lost importance as the church began to baptize at other times of the year, often within forty or even eight days of birth. The increasing frequency of taking communion only on Easter filled Holy Saturday with confessions and the Vigil moved from the middle of the night to evening then afternoon, then not at all by the end of the medieval period and the beginning of the Reformation era.

The evening hour for the Easter Vigil was restored in 1951; Vatican II made revisions to recapture this celebration for Roman Catholics. Protestant churches began following this tradition or holding sunrise services during the second half of the twentieth century. Some congregations hold the Easter Vigil during their regular Saturday evening worship time, extending it up to three hours. Others begin at 10:30 or 11:00 P.M. on Saturday, celebrating communion around midnight. *Chalice Worship* (ed. Colbert S. Cartwright and O. I. Cricket Harrison [St. Louis: Chalice, 1997]), the worship book of the Disciples of Christ/Christian Church, gives options beginning with the Vigil late Saturday evening, timed to baptize after midnight; a predawn service that begins in darkness and concludes in daylight; an early service of Light and Word, festive breakfast, service of baptism and/or reaffirmation of baptismal vows; then the regular Easter morning worship with celebration of the Lord's Supper.

The Great Fifty Days of Easter to Pentecost are the oldest and most joyful season of the Christian year, based on the events of Jesus' resurrection, his appearances to the disciples, Ascension, and the descent of the Holy Spirit. In the earliest centuries of the church, the emphasis was less on the beginning and ending days and more on the entire fifty days of celebration (see Patrick Regan, chapter 13, "The Fifty Days and the Fiftieth Day" in *BMH*). Recent theologians have called this a time to "practice resurrection." This time period matches the Jewish feast of Pentecost, the fifty days from the Feast of Unleavened Bread to the Feast of the First Fruits. During the Great Fifty Days the early church was encouraged, as signs of the resurrection, not to fast or to kneel during prayers. The book of Acts was read as proof of the resurrection and for its effects on the life of the growing church. From earliest times of the church the **Ascension** of Christ into heaven after the resurrection was celebrated either on Easter Day in the evening (Luke 24:50-53) or on the fortieth day after Easter (Acts 1:3-11), or during other points of the Great Fifty Days between Easter and Pentecost (see Stookey, *Calendar*, 173–174, n16). During the latter half of the fourth century, the celebration was stabilized on the **fortieth day** (symbolizing fullness of time or a completeness of activity) after Easter, on the Thursday between the sixth and seventh Sundays of Easter. It is often celebrated in churches on the seventh Sunday of Easter, if there are not weekday services. The primary symbolism associated with Ascension is the extinguishing of the Paschal candle, symbolizing that the risen Christ was no longer physically walking among the disciples. Some churches nowadays leave the candle lit and by the altar table until Pentecost; others move it on this day to the baptismal font.

On **Pentecost,** the followers of Jesus were gathered in Jerusalem and received the Holy Spirit (Acts 2). Other Jews were gathered as well for the Jewish feast of the fifty days after Passover, which in the first century came to commemorate both the offering of new grain (Lev 23:16) and the giving of the Law to Moses on Mount Sinai. During the earliest centuries of the church Pentecost referred to all the fifty days following Easter (Regan, "The Fifty Days and the Fiftieth Day" in *BMH*). During the times of Tertullian (ca. 160–ca. 225, African church father) and Eusebius (fourth-century bishop) there was a single day in which the ascension of Jesus and the descent of the Holy Spirit were observed; however, by the time of the Apostolic Constitution (Syria, latter half of the fourth century) Ascension was observed forty days after the resurrection and Pentecost at fifty days, following Acts 1:3. Because of the practice of baptisms on Pentecost, it is sometimes called **Whitsunday**, "white Sunday," for the robes worn by baptismal candidates.

In the Alexandrian tradition of the early church, after the celebration of the baptism of Jesus at Epiphany a fast began; this recalled Jesus' forty days in the wilderness and ended with baptisms. The church in Rome and North Africa had three weeks of preparation before Easter for those being baptized, and other parts of the early church also held three-week baptismal preparations at various times of the year. At the Council of Nicaea in 325, these fasts were combined into what we know as the season of Lent, an extended time of fasting, and Easter baptisms were linked with the images of Romans 6, the dying and rising of Christ. Maxwell E. Johnson argues, following Talley, that this means that the origins of Lent were not related to the Pascha itself but to baptismal practices. For Johnson, this suggests reconsideration of Lent's commonly held focus on "passion" to that of a more baptismal orientation ("Preparation for Pascha? Lent in Christian Antiquity," in *BMH*, 222). Throughout Christian history, Lent has varied in length because of the way the "forty days" and the ending of the fast were determined. In the West, Sundays were still little Easters and not part of the Lenten fast. In the East, both Saturday and Sunday were not fast days. All of the **fasts** included one meal a day, usually occurring at 3 P.M. or after, which avoided meat, fish, eggs, and dairy (what we today would call a vegan diet). The purposes of fasting were several: preparing to receive the Holy Spirit by those who would be baptized on

Easter, as a discipline to make room for God, and to practice caring for the poor by giving them the money one would have spent on food. The ending of Lent was considered variously as Holy Thursday, Good Friday, Holy Saturday, or the Saturday before Palm/Passion Sunday. As society in northern Europe and the Mediterranean became more and more Christian, there were fewer adult baptisms and the focus of Lent shifted during the medieval period from baptismal preparation to penitence for the whole congregation. Traditional Lenten practices include the use of purple vestments and kneeling for prayers (both symbolizing penitence), and the omissions of the word *Alleluia,* the **Gloria in excelsis**/Glory to God in the highest, weddings, and the ringing of bells. In our day in the United States, Lenten disciplines might also include cutting back on watching television, playing computer games, or surfing the Internet in order to make room for God or for baptismal candidates to prepare for receiving the Holy Spirit, and to allow more time for everyone to pray more or do more kind acts for others.

Putting on sackcloth and ashes was a sign of repentance and sorrow (e.g., Esth 4:1-3; Job 42:6; Ps 102:9; Jer 6:26; Dan 9:3; and Jonah 3:6). In the early Roman church, persons who had committed public sins and been shut away from the fellowship of the congregation had an opportunity to repent and be readmitted into the congregation each Lent. In the 600s the Western church added **Ash Wednesday** to mark out forty days of fasting (excluding Sundays) from that day through the Saturday before Easter. This day to remember our mortality and our need of God's grace has included marking with ashes since early times, first for those who needed to be reconciled with the church. Between the eighth and tenth centuries, this evolved into a general repentance by the whole congregation and its clergy, when all received the sign of ashes. Although the marking with ashes at the beginning of Lent was abandoned by the time of the

Reformation, it has been recovered in the last century as an important reminder of what we have become by our own means and what we might
yet become through the mercy of God. Egeria tells of a procession with
palm fronds from the Mount of Olives to Jerusalem in the afternoon on
the Sunday of Holy Week, what we now call **Palm/Passion Sunday**. This
was imitated in Spain in the next century and in Gaul by the seventh century. In the medieval period the procession began at one of the smaller
churches in town and processed to the cathedral; in colder climates processions took place through the churchyard and around the aisles of the
church. Palm branches were often replaced by whatever was locally available, including willow or olive branches. The Passion story has long been
read or chanted on this day, following the celebration of Jesus' entry into
Jerusalem. In places where Holy Week services are poorly attended or
omitted, it is particularly important that the crucifixion story be read on
this day.

The Incarnational Cycle:
Birth and the Sanctifying of Human Life

Epiphany, from the Greek meaning "manifestation" or "revelation," is
celebrated on January 6 or on the Sunday between January 2 and January 8. This is the third feast known to the early church—after Easter and
Pentecost—widely celebrated as early as the fourth century, for God's incarnation in Christ. It was originally filled with images of Jesus' birth, the
visit of the **Magi** or wise men, Jesus' baptism in the Jordan River by his
cousin John, and the first miracle at a wedding in Cana changing water
into wine. Over time, the Western church separated this day into multiple
celebrations, as **Christmas** (birth), **Epiphany** (visit of the Magi), and the
Baptism of Jesus Christ on the Sunday after the Epiphany. (In the *RCL*, the
reading of John 2:1-11, the wedding at Cana, appears only on the Second
Sunday after the Epiphany in Year C.) In the West, baptism in the early

church was normally connected with a post-Epiphany fast, which later develops into our season of Lent (see Paul F. Bradshaw, "The Origins of Easter," in *BMH*, 121; and Lenten discussion above). In one sense, Christmas has been taken over by the secular culture in North America, so giving Epiphany more importance might help the church recapture some of the deeper meanings of incarnation.

By the fifth century, the number of Magi becomes fixed at three, from the three gifts mentioned in Matthew 2:11. In some parts of the world, gifts are given to children on Epiphany, and in Hispanic communities La Fiesta de los Reyes Magos, or the Feast of the Three Kings, is a major winter celebration.

Christmas (Christ + Mass), the celebration in the Western Church of Jesus' birth, is a season of twelve days from December 25 through the Epiphany (following Peter G. Cobb, "The History of the Christian Year," in *The Study of Liturgy,* rev. ed., ed. Cheslyn Jones, Geoffrey Wainwright, Edward Yarnold, S.J., and Paul Bradshaw [London: Oxford University Press, 1978, 1992]; Frank C. Senn, *The People's Work: A Social History of the Liturgy* [Minneapolis: Fortress, 2006]; and Stookey, *Calendar*). Early evidence for a separate day for the birth comes from Rome around 354 and Constantinople by 380; before 311, there is a reference to possible celebration in North Africa. There are two primary theories regarding the setting of Christmas on December 25 in the Western Church (rather than the Eastern Church's celebration at Epiphany), and at this point in history both are still held. The first, often called the "history of religions theory," suggests that Christians took over a Roman secular holiday near the winter solstice. The second, called the "computation or calculation hypothesis," was posed by French Christian historian Louis Duchesne in 1889 and 1903 and revived in the twentieth century by Thomas J. Talley. The reasoning is that Jesus would have been conceived on the same date that he died; this was eventually set on March 25, and nine months later would be December 25 (see readings by Thomas J. Talley and Susan K. Roll in *BMH* for more information on these theories and the history behind them). Whichever theory you believe, it is true that some solstice observances have crept into Christmas, with trees, candles, and Yule logs. When Christmas became its own celebration in the West, it was celebrated with three services: a midnight Mass of the Angels, a dawn Mass of the Shepherds, and a midday Mass of the Incarnation (Senn, *The People's Work,* 151).

The days between Christmas and Epiphany were claimed by the church as a time to live into God's incarnation in Christ and to love the Christ in all persons. Lectionaries deal variously with these days, depending on where the Sundays fall—some move from the first Sunday after Christmas to New Year's to Epiphany; others include first and second Sundays of Christmas, Holy Name of Jesus on New Year's Day, then Epiphany. Whatever lectionary one follows, one should keep the focus on incarnation and its impact on human living.

These are the days the current church can reclaim as its own for celebration and spiritual growth as the secular world in the Northern Hemisphere takes down its decorations and moves on to the next holiday. This could be a time for your congregation to gather and celebrate each of the holy days, or you might simply pay attention to the Sundays and make sure that they contain the full joy of Incarnation, rather than the "letdown" time after Christmas that the secular world experiences. If a holy day falls on a Sunday, consider the option of focusing on it instead of the regular Sunday readings (see chapter 5 for additional ideas).

January 1 has been celebrated in various ways throughout the history of the church, first as a celebration of Mary, then for the Circumcision of Jesus (Luke 2:21, the eighth day after Christmas) or **Feast of the Holy**

Name. The celebration of New Year's Day is actually a late church celebration, beginning throughout northern Europe in 1752 when the Grego-
rian calendar was adopted. Previously, Advent served as the beginning of
the year in many places; other places celebrated some indication of the
coming spring in the Northern Hemisphere; and in still other places March
25 marked the new year because of the **Annunciation,** or conception of
Jesus. The celebration of circumcision and the giving of Jesus' name are
events that marked his entrance into the Hebrew faith. The celebration of
the new year is a reminder that for Christians every day is New Year's Day,
when we are forgiven the past and called to live a new life in Jesus Christ.

The development of **Advent** (from Latin, *adventus,* "coming") as a season of preparation for Christmas has a varied path in the Western Church.
The Council of Saragossa (Spain, 380) noted that no one was permitted
to be absent from church between December 17 through the day of
Epiphany (Louis Duchesne, *Christian Worship* [London: SPCK, 1923],
260n. 3). The Synod of Tours in 567, Pope Gregory the Great (540–604),
and Bede (ca. 673–735) each mention forty days of preparation and fasting, often beginning around November 11. The Gelasian Sacramentary
(mid-700s, Gaul) speaks of a season of six Sundays before Christmas. The
four weeks we know now as Advent were stable by the time of the *Book
of Common Prayer* (1549) and the *Roman Missal* (1570). During Advent,
there was fasting and the "Gloria in excelsis" was not sung; but unlike
Lent, alleluias were permitted. Today Advent is celebrated as a season of
expectant and joyful longing for the fulfillment of God's promised reign,
as we wait for the One who has already come (Ministry Unit on Theology and Worship for the Presbyterian Church (USA) and the Cumberland
Presbyterian Church, *Liturgical Year: The Worship of God, Supplemental Liturgical Resource* 7 [Louisville: Westminster John Knox, 1992], 280).

Currently there is debate in a number of different places in North America about the length and placement of Advent and Christmas, given the overwhelming consumer orientation at the onset of Christmas decorations and sales at the beginning of November. Marva J. Dawn, in *A Royal "Waste" of Time: The Splendor of Worshiping God and Being Church for the World,* argues for keeping the current four-Sunday pattern as it requires us to live counterculturally, teaches waiting and patience, and challenges us to live for God's reign rather than for current society (Grand Rapids: Eerdmans, 1999, 280–282). Churches who continue the current pattern need to work hard to stay in peaceful waiting mode in Advent and then add energy to the celebration of Incarnation during the twelve days of Christmas, December 25 through January 5. These later dates would be the time to schedule Christmas concerts, programs, and parties at church. These congregations may also delay setting up Christmas decorations (greenery; a Chrismon or Christmas tree; nativity scene, or crèche) until December 24. See chapter 3 for suggestions about music during the Advent season.

The Advent Project with William H. Petersen and others from the North American Academy of Liturgy, an ecumenical group of liturgical scholars, has been working since 2007 for the expansion of Advent to seven weeks. They argue that observing Advent for seven weeks is more like the earlier Advent, matches the practice of Advent in the Orthodox Church, needs no revision of the *Revised Common Lectionary,* fights secular consumerism, and gives appropriate focus on Christ and eschatology.

Taylor Burton-Edwards and others currently at the United Methodist General Board of Discipleship acknowledge the tendency in U.S. churches to lose people in worship attendance after Christmas Eve and so suggests moving Advent to begin two weeks earlier, thus freeing up the two Sundays before Christmas for focus on the Incarnational texts usually missed during the Sundays after Christmas (http://www.gbod.org/site/apps/nlnet/content3.aspx?c=nhLRJ2PMKsG&b=5302879&ct=3834769).

This book stays with the current status of a four-Sunday Advent, suggesting that this is a place for practicing Christian counterculturalism, and working harder to involve the church in the days between Christmas and Epiphany.

Ordinary Time after the Epiphany

Ordinary Time receives its name from the use of ordinal numbers (1st, 2nd, 3rd, etc.) used to count the Sundays after the Epiphany and, earlier, after Pentecost, the two "seasons" of Ordinary Time. Each season of Ordinary Time begins and ends with a special Sunday.

The time after Epiphany begins with **Baptism of Christ Sunday**. As Stookey has pointed out in *Calendar* (112, 158), the thread that connects Christmas, Epiphany, and Baptism of Christ is the identification of the child of Bethlehem as God's Anointed One. Many congregations celebrate this day by remembering and reaffirming their baptismal vows.

The last Sunday before Lent, the Sunday before Ash Wednesday is known as **Transfiguration Sunday**. This day celebrates the event told in Matthew 17:1-13; Mark 9:2-13; and Luke 9:28-36, and referred to in 2 Peter 1:16-18, when Jesus was transfigured, with Moses and Elijah appearing on either side of him. Long celebrated in the Eastern Church on August 6, and in the Western Church since the fifteenth century, the *RCL* followed Lutheran tradition in setting Transfiguration as the last Sunday of the season after the Epiphany, as the culmination of this season of light, and marking Jesus setting his face to go to Jerusalem (Luke 9:51) as we move into Lent. Its alternative Latin name, **Quinquagesima** Sunday, refers to its placement fifty (Quinqua-) days before Easter and is the name seen in many older church calendars.

The first Sunday after Pentecost, **Trinity Sunday,** is unusual in that it is not primarily a celebration of a Christological event but of the triune God, who is with us and for us always. It was first celebrated in the 1000s, then made an official feast day in the West in 1344 and placed on the Sunday after Pentecost. Since Ordinary Time follows Trinity Sunday, the counting of Sundays has often been: the __ Sunday after Trinity or the __ Sunday after Pentecost (Trinity equaling the first Sunday after Pentecost) and is now often simply named as a date (July x–x) in Ordinary Time, for example, in the *RCL*.

The final Sunday after Pentecost, the Sunday before Advent begins, is **Reign of Christ** or **Christ the King Sunday**. This day was the last to be instituted into the Christian year, set in 1925 by Pope Pius XI, and moved to the last Sunday before Advent in the Roman Calendar of 1969 and the *Common Lectionary*. This Sunday functions as the turning point from Ordinary Time, looking back to Christ's glory at Transfiguration, Easter, and Ascension, and forward to Christ's coming again in glory as our sovereign at Advent, Christmas, and Epiphany. With this placement it is a day to celebrate the reign of the risen Christ over all things and all time.

Ordinary Time after Pentecost from May or June through November is the longest season in the Christian year, which has resulted in both special Sundays within its time and occasional suggestions of other ways of dividing this time (on the latter, see chapter 5).

October 1 or the first Sunday in October is celebrated in many Protestant churches as **World Communion Sunday**. This observance began in the Presbyterian Church (USA) and abroad in 1936 and quickly spread through the denominations of the Federal Council of Churches, now known as the National Council of Churches. With the increasing acknowledgment of globalization in our time, World Communion is an important bond among Christians.

November 1 or the first Sunday in November is celebrated in many congregations as **All Saints**. As early as 400 there was an annual feast for known and unknown **martyrs,** those who had died for their Christian beliefs, celebrated on various dates after Easter. Eventually in the Western Church, observation settled on November 1 with prayers of thanks for all the official saints of the church. November 2, called **All Souls Day**, remembered all the faithful departed (not just the official saints), and was celebrated through the medieval period. During the Reformation, these two days were combined in the Protestant Church and celebrated to thank God for the examples of those who have gone before. (For information on the secular traditions that preceded All Saints in Celtic Britain and Ireland and the echoes of those traditions still in the secular Halloween [from hallowed evening] of our day, see Senn, *The People's Work*, 79, 166, and 201.)

Throughout Christian history there is evidence of thank offerings of first fruits (Num. 18:8-32), particularly during the Northern Hemisphere fall harvests. The most common occasion in the medieval period was the feast of St. Martin of Tours, celebrated on November 11, which continued in many places even after the Reformation. It has been suggested that this tradition is what the Pilgrims drew on when they introduced a day of **Thanksgiving** into their lives in North America ("Harvest Thanksgiving," in *The New Westminster Dictionary of Liturgy and Worship,* ed. Paul Bradshaw [Louisville: Westminster John Knox, 2002]). Some churches join together across denominational lines, while some join with other faiths, as this is something we share in common—giving thanks to the Source of All Good Gifts, by whatever name we use. This day is celebrated on the fourth Thursday in November in the United States and on the second Monday in October in Canada.

Missio Dei

Definition

The phrase **missio Dei** has become important in the discussion of mission in Christianity, particularly over the last fifty years. As described by

David J. Bosch in *Transforming Mission,* "Mission is not primarily an activity of the church but an attribute of God" (Maryknoll, N.Y.: Orbis, 1991, 390). God is a sending God, so that mission is a movement from God to the world. The biblical model of missio Dei connects with the worship of the church, 1 Peter 2:9: "But you are a chosen race, a royal priesthood, a holy nation, God's own people, in order that you may proclaim the mighty acts of the One who called you out of darkness into God's own marvelous light" (paraphrased). We are called to worship God in order that we might proclaim God's mighty acts and the transformation God has made in our lives. In worship we are formed into God's sent people, more and more ready and equipped to work with God in the world. These formational aspects of worship, sustained by passing on the traditions of the faith and frequent repetition, are energized each week by God's sending us out into today's world in the light of that day's particular scriptures.

Some congregations in the United States have experimented on Sunday mornings with mission events (feeding the hungry, working on homes for the homeless) instead of worship. Yet it is impossible for human beings to take part in missio Dei without constantly being nourished and formed by time with God and one another in communal worship; too much reliance on our own "good deeds" can burn us out quickly if we are not rooted and grounded in God. In the work that follows, missio Dei has shaped the worship elements through the lens of 1 Peter 2:9, with continual reminders that we are chosen by God, made holy by God, made into a royal priesthood through baptism, and sent as God's own people to proclaim God's mighty acts throughout history and in our lives and the life of the world. Yet worship alone cannot form and send us; it needs to be part of the church's whole life together that includes study and mission activities.

Year in Brief with Broad Missional Strokes

Christmas-Epiphany and Advent: Incarnation is the action of God coming in human form to demonstrate how much the world is loved, how much all human life is valued, and what a holy life looks like. We are the body of Christ, sent to show every person how much he or she is loved and valued, and to demonstrate the many ways to embody a holy life. Incarnation also points out God's care for our daily lives, desiring that all persons have their basic needs for shelter, food, health, and love met; thus it is appropriate for the church to be concerned about these needs of the world as well.

The Triduum (Holy Thursday, Good Friday, and Easter), the Great Fifty Days, Pentecost, Lent: Sin is inevitable, and an innocent and holy man, Jesus, was put to death, without protest or argument. Then resurrection came and turned everything upside down. We live in a postresurrection, Spirit-filled world; Christ has overcome fear and death to show God's amazing mercy and unfathomable love. Love and grace are now the law. This can clash with the laws of the land, and Christians are repeatedly called to stand up for God's laws of justice, love, and grace.

Ordinary Time, after the Epiphany and after Pentecost: Framed by incarnation and resurrection, God calls us to take love into the world where God is at work. We are called in our lives every day to help God's will be done on earth as it is in heaven. We are called to love each person God puts in our path, to reach out to the outcast, to dare to live God's ways, to decenter ourselves and center on God. Decentering ourselves forces us to call into question our loyalties and the idols that beckon us from putting and keeping God first; selfless love and living naturally involve us in the lives of the world and institutions around us, seeking to help them be more Christlike, just, and grace-filled.

Hymns for Missio Dei, Can Be Used at Any Time during the Christian

Year: Choose one for a season and let it become formational, part of your congregation's heart language.

As a fire is meant for burning (Duck)

Enviado soy de Dios/Sent Out in Jesus' Name (anon.)

Go forth for God (Peacey)

In the midst of new dimensions (Rush)

Lord, whose love through humble service (Bayly)

Lord, you give the great commission (Rowthorn)

May the God of hope go with us every day/Canto de Esperanza
(Schutmaat)

Send me, Lord (trad. South African)

Shalom to you now, shalom, my friends (Eslinger)

The kingdom of God is justice and peace (Taizé)

The Spirit sends us forth to serve (Dufner)

We all are one in mission (Edwards)

PLANNING WORSHIP

Planning by season helps us see parallels in the rituals and symbols that reappear in new ways.

Some Parallels within the Christian Year

Candle-lighting: The focus on light in the first part of the Easter Vigil derives from the Jewish tradition of lighting candles for Sabbath, interpreted by the early church, at the lighting of the evening lamps, into thanksgiving for Christ as the light of the world. This evolved into congregational candle lighting at the vigils on the evenings prior to baptisms at Epiphany, Easter, and Pentecost. In the early centuries of the church, in Jerusalem at the Pascha, the bishop would emerge from the tomb of Christ with lighted tapers, proclaiming the resurrection of Christ. The **Paschal candle,** or **Easter**

candle, is larger than any other candles used in the church and traditionally is decorated with the Greek letters Alpha (A) and Omega (Ω) (symbolizing Christ, the first and last) and the current year numerals (symbolizing that the Christ of the ages is present here and now); it remains lit during the Great Fifty Days by the altar table (or is moved to the baptismal font after Ascension) and is also lit at baptisms and funerals.

On Christmas Eve, most congregations in North America sing "Silent Night" by **candlelight** (although some use battery candles instead of flames due to fire concerns). The light is carried from the altar table or from a Christ candle in the middle of the Advent wreath to ushers or acolytes and then to the congregation. Some congregations lift their candles during the final stanza of the singing or benediction, then blow them out, turn up the sanctuary lights, and sing "Joy to the World" as a sending forth.

The **Advent wreath** began as a home devotion in Reformation Germany and traveled north into churches during the second half of the 1900s. The candles help us mark the coming of God Incarnate; focusing on concepts or persons with the candles or giving them names (e.g., the joy candle or the Mary candle) loses the sense of movement toward Incarnation through the symbol of increasing light. The use of one pink candle among the purple comes from the older tradition of a somber and penitential Advent, with the third Sunday (**Gaudete,** or rejoicing) being a break for joy. Since Advent is becoming more distinct from Lent, it is appropriate and simpler to have all four candles be blue for the hope of God's coming. Some congregations switch to all white candles for Christmas Eve; others remove the wreath entirely and simply have a large Christ candle.

Many monasteries of the medieval period observed a **Tenebrae** or Service of Shadows during Holy Week on Wednesday through Friday (*Liturgical Year,* 301). Today some churches observe this ritual during Holy

Week or spread it throughout Lent. Tenebrae essentially reverses the adding of lights in Advent as we approach Christmas; in Lent we gradually extinguish the light as we approach Good Friday. Like the Advent wreath, Tenebrae is often surrounded by scripture reading and prayer.

Cross: The cross is the central symbol for the Christian faith and almost always found in worship spaces. During Lent some congregations switch their gold cross for a wooden one. Throughout the Christian year, particularly in the seasons of Christmas-Epiphany and the Great Fifty Days, consider featuring one of the wooden crosses from El Salvador, which have been covered with pictures of life in Christ. While the cross carries the symbolism of the martyrdom of Christ, the vibrant colors and joyful incarnational images of God's people found on the Salvadoran crosses remind us of Christ's abundant life (see "Cross of the Community" by artisans of La Palma, El Salvador, in *Imaging the Word: An Arts and Lectionary Resource* [IW], ed. Susan A. Blain [Cleveland: United Church Press, 1995], 2:81).

Processions: Processions of clergy, acolytes, choir, cross, Bible, and even congregation are natural elements of worship, symbolizing the journey we are on with God. On festival Sundays and holy days—Palm Sunday (waving palm branches), Easter, Christmas Eve, and Epiphany—processions add a joyful solemnity to worship. There is also a tradition of processing with the cross on Good Friday and then with the Paschal candle at the Easter Vigil, with congregational responses at three points of the journey—back of the sanctuary, middle, and then by the altar table.

Conflicts with the Secular Calendar

The secular calendar comes into conflict fairly often with the liturgical year and so the church must continue to choose whom it will serve—businesses with investments in Christmas sales and Mother's and Father's

Days, the patriotic holidays of the nation (Memorial Day, Veterans Day, and July 4th in the United States) or the continuing story of salvation through Jesus Christ. This particularly becomes an issue as calendars conflict around the celebration of Pentecost, with Mother's Day, Memorial Day, and the honoring of high school graduates. Congregations with heavy investment in the secular culture can feel ignored if worship does not honor the things that the culture honors. Yet it is always the task of the church to call us back to God's values and God's big story, within which our culture's story and our own little story fit. While this book suggests that the Christian calendar should always take precedence over the secular calendar, there is often a way to offer gentle reminders when secular calendar conflicts arise. For example, consider affirming on Mother's Day and Father's Day the new family we have in Christ through baptism, where we nourish and encourage one another to grow, bound together by the Holy Spirit rather than by biology. Consider national holidays through the perspective of God's vision—how has our country lived up to God's ideals? What work still needs to be done? (See also Richard L. Eslinger, "Civil Religion and the Year of Grace," in *Worship* 58:4 [July 1984]: 372–383.)

Actual Planning

As you plan for worship, are there persons in the congregation with skills that would enrich your worship life? Open your search to include persons of all ages, longtime members and those new to the community, persons with fully developed gifts and persons with possibilities. Worship together, pray together, and then work together that your worship life together might be rich and full.

The basic pattern of worship received from the early church and followed by many churches today is fourfold: Gathering, Word, Table, and

Sending Forth. Begin your planning by gathering worship books, hymnals, and calendars for several months. Consider the discussions of missio Dei in this book and the hymns, songs, and spirituals given for seasons and holy days to supplement your congregation's favorites. Focus on a scripture for the liturgical season or holy day, or a theme. Follow a creative process that begins with prayer and gives time for gathering ideas and images. Sometimes resources that you select may need adapting for your particular worshiping community; pay attention to your congregation's heart language. For each worship experience, consider first how the Word will be proclaimed and heard, then how the congregation may be involved in responding, and how they will be sent back into the world. That process will direct your subsequent planning for the gathering time. Whether you are planning whole services from scratch or simply making adaptations to your current service, understanding the movement of worship gives a good foundation. Finally, as you began your worship planning with prayer, give thanks as you end and then plan to gather as worship leaders to pray together again before the actual service begins (Robin Knowles Wallace, *Worshiping in the Small Membership Church* [Nashville: Abingdon, 2008], 69).

This book lists a variety of names and adjectives appropriate for God by season and holy day. They are provided that you might include them in praying or preaching in worship to broaden the understanding of God for your congregation.

One question that often arises around the lectionary is whether it needs to be followed exclusively. The suggestion of this book is that yes, the Paschal and Incarnational cycles are vital and need to pass on the life-giving practices of the Christian faith. But, no, particularly in Ordinary Time, there is room for expansion into other emphases, such as heroines and heroes of the scriptures, or the Minor Prophets or Pastoral Epistles.

Color

Color is an important and simple way to mark the change of the seasons. In general, Christological festivals—Easter, Christmas, and Epiphany—are white and gold for celebration. Preparatory seasons—Lent and Advent— were purple for penitence and the royalty of Jesus Christ; now most often Advent is blue for hope. In many churches, that means when the purple Advent paraments are worn out or money becomes available there is a move to obtain blue Advent paraments.

Days of the Holy Spirit—Pentecost and ordinations—are red. Ordinary seasons are green, and each is marked by a beginning and ending Sunday, which is white—Baptism of Christ Jesus, Transfiguration Sunday, Trinity Sunday, and Reign of Christ Sunday. All Saints' Day is white, as are funerals and baptisms. Good Friday may have no color, or be red or black. Note that color meanings change by culture; these given are standard for North America and Europe. Within any season the shades may vary, often intensifying as the season progresses.

Music

Music has an important role in enabling praise, teaching theological truths, challenging our thinking, and drawing us together as a community. Singing together is a disappearing art in much of the Northern Hemisphere, and Christian churches are some of the last places where people are regularly expected and willing to be vulnerable enough to sing. There are tensions within congregations between building a broad repertoire of hymnody or allowing congregations to repeat songs they know and love. The hymn, song, and spiritual choices in this book attempt to provide a mix of the many new options in hymnody (particularly songs that are not yet in denominational hymnals), some traditional hymns, and some music from around the world, all chosen for intergenerational singing, to supplement your congregation's favorites. When songs are appropriate for scriptures throughout a season or series of Sundays, don't be afraid to repeat the song; what we know well becomes part of our theological understanding and heart language.

While texts are very important for teaching theology and expressing our faith, it is the tune that determines for most people whether the hymn is "singable." On the hymnal page, along with the tune name, you will also find its meter, either a series of numbers (such as 86.86) or letters (CM, SM, Irr., etc.). The meter is the number of syllables that each line of the hymn text contains. English meters include:

CM = Common Meter = 86.86

SM = Short Meter = 66.86

LM = Long Meter = 88.88

D = double, meaning that the meter pattern occurs twice in each stanza; for example, CMD = 86.86 times two, or 86.86.86.86 for each stanza or verse

Irr. = Irregular, generally meters that are so unusual that there is only one match for each text/tune

As you learn which tunes your congregation knows, write down the tune name and its meter. Most likely there will be a variety of meters represented and some meters with multiple tunes. For example, under CM, you may have AZMON, a tune for "O for a thousand tongues to sing" and AMAZING GRACE (also called NEW BRITAIN). Since they share a meter, that means that the words to "Amazing Grace" can be sung to the tune of "O for a thousand tongues to sing" and vice versa. Try it and see how the texts and tunes fit together, and also how a different tune gives the text a different feel.

The doubling of some texts or tunes adds other interesting possibilities. When the tune is doubled, with eight lines, two verses of a four-line text fit it. When the text is eight lines, sing a four-line tune twice to fit the text. When there are an odd number of verses, use half of the tune or repeat a stanza to make things come out even.

This key can multiply your worship music repertoire exponentially!

• Sing new texts to familiar tunes instead of unknown tunes, thus encouraging more confident singing from the congregation. Printing the text as poetry, rather than interlined between music staves, assists this process; consider using public domain texts or purchase a copyright license for your congregation.

• Switch known texts and tunes within the same meter to add freshness to the text. As variation, use doubled tunes with texts.

• Use a text without refrain to the tune of the same meter that has a refrain. An example of this would be singing the text of either "Amazing Grace" or "O for a thousand tongues to sing" to the tune of the verse of "O How I Love Jesus" (CM with refrain) and then singing the refrain "O how I love Jesus."

• Learn a new tune that has a meter that can be used for multiple texts and then sing the tune frequently until it becomes part of the repertoire of the congregation.

• As you switch texts and tunes, pay attention to the mood of the tune so that the text matches appropriately (Wallace, *Worshiping in the Small Membership Church*, 103–105).

How to Use This Book

Throughout this book, hymns are listed by first line or common title and author; composers are not listed due to space. Websites for finding new hymns include Hope Hymnody Online, http://www.hopepublishing. com/html/main.isx?sitesec=40.0.0.1; HymnPrint.net, http://www.hymn print.net/; and Hymnary.org, http://www.hymnary.org/.

Things in the public domain may be reprinted or projected for free; things in copyright require a one-time usage payment or a copyright license such as OneLicense, http://www.onelicense.net/ (mainline, GIA [Roman Catholic and other liturgical sources], Taizé, and Iona music); or CCLI, http://www.ccli.com/ (contemporary praise and worship, primarily; some mainline and liturgical) or LicenSing (primarily mainline, more international), available through Logos Productions in the United States, http://www.logosproductions.com/, Wood Lake Publishing, Inc. in Canada, http://www.woodlakebooks.com, or MediaCom Education, Inc. in Australia, http://www.mediacom.org.au/. All African American spirituals noted are in the public domain, and in traditional practice can have verses subtracted or added as appropriate.

PREACHING

Preaching is an important means of encountering God in worship through the preacher's preparation and the work of the Holy Spirit. Preaching is naming moments of grace in scripture and in the world around us, so that the congregation can go out and see God's work in the world and witness to it. Preaching is formational: it shapes our daily lives, reminding us of God's promises kept and helping us draw nearer to God. Preaching is missional: it energizes and sends the congregation to be Christ's body in the world. Preaching is prophetic: it reminds us that we live in the world where God is incarnate and resurrected yet where abuse and oppression are strong and always to be resisted. Preaching is contextual: it is directed to the congregation assembled, to their daily lives, and both to the world that they see and the world that they are overlooking.

Preaching should be an engaging encounter, whether with words, visuals, drama, narrative, silence, or sounds. Emerging churches, small-membership churches, and others are working with the ideas of

participatory preaching, where the preacher frames the scriptures by giving context and history, and then the congregation, either as a whole or in small groups, talks about how the scriptures intersect with their daily lives. Rather than relieving the preacher of exegetical work and deep thought, this style of participatory preaching invites the congregation to strengthen their own work with scripture and its application to their lives.

At times in the recent history of the church, preaching has had to bear all the weight of encountering God in worship. Studies of the early church, of symbol and sacrament, of the various ways human beings learn and experience God, all suggest that there are many ways to encounter God in worship and that preaching is one important, weekly way to do so. Preachers should also be worship leaders, able to give energy to the various elements of worship and open themselves to encounter God while leading worship.

Each section of this book on a season or holy day includes thoughts about the focus of preaching and often resources for inspiration—particularly poetry. See also Mary Catherine Hilkert's *Naming Grace: Preaching and the Sacramental Imagination* (New York: Continuum, 1997); Lucy Lind Hogan's *Graceful Speech: An Invitation to Preaching* (Louisville: Westminster John Knox, 2006); Bill Kellermann's *Seasons of Faith and Conscience: Kairos, Confession, Liturgy (Seasons)* (Maryknoll, N.Y.: Orbis, 1991); sermons by Barbara Brown Taylor (in her collections *God in Pain: Teaching Sermons on Suffering* [Nashville: Abingdon, 1998]; *Home by Another Way* [Cambridge, Mass.: Cowley, 1999]; *Mixed Blessings* [Atlanta: S. Hunter, 1986]); and Stookey's *Calendar.*

Prayer for Sermon Preparation

O God who gives words of eternal life,
inspire my heart with life-giving words,
that your people here at [name of church]
will come to know you better;

in the name of your Word—preached, believed, and incarnate.

Amen. (Michele Lynne Holloway)

SUMMARY

The Christian or liturgical year is an important practice for Christians as it draws us into an encounter with God through Christ and the Holy Spirit in ways that mirror human life—birth, death, suffering, joy, ordinary and extraordinary days. The development of the Christian year throughout history was no single trajectory, but rather a variety of practices and times that people found appropriate, which then converged and were agreed upon or continued to be celebrated in divergent ways. One important advantage in this day of globalization is that following the liturgical year unites Christians across the globe even though we may be divided by many other things. Using the *Revised Common Lectionary* unites congregations in North America and other places across denominational lines, especially in the holy seasons of Incarnation and Resurrection.

God is a sending God who calls us to the work and joy of missio Dei, God's own reign and vision for creation. Worship can be formational and varied, not only gathering us and forming us as the body of Christ, but, more important, sending us with joy to do the will of God in the world, to love the outcast as Jesus did, and to point to where the Holy Spirit is at work in our world.

CHAPTER 2

THE PASCHAL CYCLE

THE TRIDUUM, EASTER-GREAT FIFTY DAYS-PENTECOST, LENT

INTRODUCTION

We begin with the earliest known holy days after the celebration of Sunday, those days of the Triduum (Holy Thursday evening through Easter day), followed by the Great Fifty Days and Pentecost, then move back to the preparatory season of Lent.

Because missio Dei is about sending, this chapter and the next two will begin with seasonal thoughts about missio Dei, and include closing words for that season's services. Missio Dei is both about sending and about how we are formed as God's people, the body of Christ. There are many forms for the closing words of worship, generally known as the **benediction**. In this book, in order to be clear about the focus on missio Dei, the format used consists of a **blessing** to be given by the pastor and a **sending** or dismissal, which may be said by a deacon, lay leader, or the pastor.

Missio Dei and the Triduum/through the Easter Vigil

The worship service during the Triduum is conceived as one long service, with a prelude and opening on Holy/Maundy Thursday and closing words and postlude following the Easter Vigil or first service of Easter. Missio Dei foci for worship elements on Holy/Maundy Thursday include the humble action of foot washing and the strengthening presence of the communion table, and for Good Friday, the intercession of Jesus for the whole world. The Easter Vigil celebrates the remarkable transformation of the world by the risen Christ, and it is this service that contains the blessing and sending.

Blessing: May God of our baptismal covenant, Christ of the cross, and Spirit of resurrection bless and transform your life.

Sending: Go to the world, conveying the transforming love of the risen Christ.

Missio Dei and the Great Fifty Days

Barbara Brown Taylor in *Christianity Today* ("The Day We Were Left Behind," http://www.ctlibrary.com/ct/1998/may18/8t6046.html) reminds us that the mission focus of Ascension, and indeed of this resurrection season, is that "followers became leaders, the listeners became preachers, the converts became missionaries, the healed became healers.... And nothing was ever the same again."

Blessing

May God, who raised Christ from the dead, help you stand again.

May Christ, who rose from the dead and ascended into heaven,

    be present with you.

May the Holy Spirit give you the courage you need

    to be God's witness in the world.

May the Holy Trinity grant you love.

Sending

Stand up and bless our God! Through all your thoughts and actions this week, witness to the power of resurrection life.

Missio Dei and Lent

Lent's focus on baptism and Christian vocation gives us an opportunity to reconsider our baptismal vows and our own entrance into the ministry of Jesus Christ, as well as into his death and resurrection. This is the season of acknowledging God's claim on our lives and relinquishing our own claims and the claims we allow the world to make on us. Considering our sin during Lent, both individual and corporate, is only possible because we know the promise of God's forgiveness and the work of Jesus on the cross. Practicing forgiveness is an excellent Lenten discipline. The cleansing of our lives and the healing of our hearts that come from God's forgiveness sets us free to be about God's work in the world: loving God and neighbor. This season moves us from despair to hope.

Blessing

May God, who knows your sins and still loves you,

      grant you freedom through forgiveness.

May Jesus Christ, who walked the hard road of human life,

      give you peace in the midst of struggle.

May the Holy Spirit, given to you in baptism,

      strengthen you for forgiving others and for loving.

May the Holy Trinity guide your way.

Sending

Go into the wilderness that is our world

      and proclaim the deep mercy of God.

THE TRIDUUM: HOLY/MAUNDY THURSDAY, GOOD FRIDAY, EASTER—THREE HOLY DAYS

Holy/Maundy Thursday

Preparation

The Lord's Supper has the central place at this service, rather than a reenactment of the Last Supper. Some congregations like to celebrate this meal in a fellowship hall seated around tables or with the congregation in a circle passing the elements and serving one another (teach words for distribution). However you celebrate communion on this day, observe two caveats: (1) don't count off into tables of twelve, and (2) don't try to re-create or appropriate a Jewish Seder. Both ignore the broader and eschatological meanings of communion that are important as we face the cross and resurrection, and the second is particularly problematic as it attempts to co-opt another religion's ritual and celebrates the Passover instead of salvation through Jesus Christ. (For further reading on these issues, see the Ministry Unit on Theology and Worship for the Presbyterian Church (USA) and the Cumberland Presbyterian Church, *The Liturgical Year: The Worship of God, Supplemental Liturgical Resource 7* [Louisville: Westminster John Knox, 1992], 37; Laurence Hull Stookey, *Calendar: Christ's Time for the Church* [Nashville: Abingdon, 1996], 92–93; J. Dudley Weaver, *Presbyterian Worship: A Guide for Clergy* [Geneva Press, 2002], 94–95.)

The important thing to remember today in recapturing the element of Christ's ministry of **foot washing** is not the act itself, which was an everyday occurrence in Jesus' day, but the doing of menial tasks by those considered more privileged, that is, servanthood. Prepare your congregation for participation in foot washing by discussing the biblical model and beginning with a demonstration the first year. Prepare a sufficient number of chairs, pitchers of warm water, accompanying basins, and plenty of towels. Place a basin under the feet, pour water over the feet into the basin, wash the feet with the hands, dry the feet with a towel, and assist with putting footwear back on. After having your own feet washed, turn and wash someone else's feet. Some congregations attempt to wash hands instead of feet, but in this season that is rather close to Pilate's washing his hands of the decision to crucify Jesus. For an alternative ritual to foot washing, see Heather Murray Elkins, "A Service of Basins and Towels" (*Holy Stuff of*

Life, Cleveland: Pilgrim, 2006). Anyone serving communion needs to wash their hands after foot washing.

Some churches prefer the color white for this evening, but purple may still be in the background. Symbols include wheat stalks, grapes, bread, cup, and, if foot washing is being done, a basin, pitcher, and towel. There is a wide variety of artwork from around the world that portrays the events of this evening, including Ernesto Cardenal's *The Gospel in Solentiname* (trans. Donald D. Walsh [Maryknoll, N.Y.: Orbis, 1982, originally four volumes], in 2010 in one volume) and "The Washing of the Feet" from the Cameroon Vie de Jesus Mafa (ed. Susan A. Blain, *Imaging the Word* [*IW*] [Cleveland: United Church Press, 1996], 3:184).

Scriptures

A, B, C: Exod. 12:1-4, (5-10), 11-14; Ps. 116:1-2, 12-19; 1 Cor. 11:23-26; John 13:1-17, 31b-35

Elements of Worship

Names and Adjectives for God, Particularly Appropriate for This Day

Beloved Jesus	Jesus, betrayed by a friend
Bread of Life	Jesus, executed by the authorities
Giver of grace	Servant of all
Giver of the New Covenant	Washer of our dirty feet, Cleanser of our dirty souls

Hymns, Songs, and Spirituals

An upper room did our Lord prepare (Pratt Green)

In remembrance of me (Courtney and Red)

Jesu, Jesu, fill us with your love (Colvin)

Jesus took the bread (Duck)

Let us break bread together on our knees (spiritual)

Love consecrates the humblest act (McManus)

Stay with me, remain here with me (Taizé [for vigil])

Ubi caritas (Taizé, one of the oldest known liturgical texts for this day)

What wondrous love is this? (U.S. folk hymn)

Agnus Dei/Lamb of God, traditionally sung before communion, is drawn from John 1:29 and reflects Isaiah 53:7. It has been used regularly in worship since the early sixth century, in musical settings as well as spoken:

Lamb of God, who takes away the sin of the world, **have mercy on us.**

Lamb of God, who takes away the sin of the world, **have mercy on us.**

Lamb of God, who takes away the sin of the world,

   grant us your peace.

Litany

Response, by all: **This is a night to remember** .... (*before each reader*)

Reader 1: With joy, for the gathering of friends and disciples around Jesus, and here among us.

Reader 2: With sadness, as it becomes clear it will be Jesus' last earthly meal with them before he is killed.

Reader 1: With joy, for the promise that Jesus is present whenever we break bread in his name.

Reader 2: With sadness, that we are no better than those of Jesus' day who misunderstood his message and betrayed him.

Reader 1: With joy, that we have known such a friend.

Reader 2: With sadness, that, like the disciples, we can't even stay awake and pray with Jesus.

Reader 1: With joy that remembers the exodus of the Hebrew people from bondage and slavery to the Promised Land.

Reader 2: With sadness that, like Peter, we too lack the courage to stand up and claim to be followers of Jesus.

Readers 1 and 2: This is a night to remember, a bittersweet time.

All: Jesus, you are our life-giving blood;

Jesus, you are the bread that sustains our bodies and hearts.

Stripping of the chancel may be done quietly during the reading of Psalm 22. It is appropriate to end this evening with a prayer vigil as Jesus asks the disciples to "watch and pray."

Preaching

Let the symbols of communion and/or foot washing speak. Brother Alois, current leader of the Taizé Community, says about Jesus washing the disciples' feet, "God's omnipotence is that of love. Jesus has 'overcome the world' (John 16:33), not by being stronger than it, but by introducing into humanity a different force, something absolutely new.... God's power is an energy of love that operates from within, gently. It can transform the harshest realities, even death" (http://www.taize.fr/en_article8367.html).

Good Friday

Preparation

This is potentially the most dramatic day of the Christian year, the day on which the One we follow died a cruel death, and as such it has many inherent tensions: divine-human, communal-individual, in church-out in society, assurance of personal salvation-day of intercession for the world, theological understandings-emotional responses, rejection, betrayal, violence, execution, and mourning, along with the question of who is to blame for the death of Jesus of Nazareth. (See preaching suggestions below for thoughts on this final tension.)

The traditional color has been black; although blood red and the grays of shadows have also been used; if the stripping of the chancel has been done, there will be no added colors in this area. If you are looking to add more artwork than just a cross, consider Georgia O'Keeffe's "Black Cross,

New Mexico" (1929), found in *IW* (3:188). Another traditional symbol for this day is the flower of the dogwood tree.

Scriptures

A, B, C: Isa. 52:13-53:12; Ps. 22; Heb. 10:16-25 or Heb. 4:14-16; 5:7-9; John 18:1–19:42

Elements and Orders of Worship

Names and Adjectives for God That Are Particularly Appropriate for This Day

Bearer of our sin	Ruler of every heart
Eternal Word of God	Suffering Servant
Holy Innocent	Vulnerable One
Reconciler	

Hymns, Songs, and Spirituals

Jesus walked this lonesome valley (U.S. folk hymn)

O sacred Head, now wounded (anonymous)

The cross on the hill is the measuring rod (Troeger)

They crucified my Lord (spiritual)

This dreadful cross of rough-hewn wood (Tice)

Were you there when they crucified my Lord? (spiritual)

What wondrous love is this? (U.S. folk hymn)

Call to Worship with Processional Cross

Leader, at the back of the sanctuary: Behold the cross on which was hung the salvation of the whole world.

(silent procession halfway to the altar table)

Leader: Behold the cross on which was hung the salvation of the whole world.

(silent procession, cross put into place by the altar table)

Leader: Behold the cross on which was hung the salvation of the whole world. Come, let us worship.

Litany or Prayer Responses

> Save us, God.
>
> Through the cross, salvation has come to the whole world.

Trisagion/Three Times Holy is used regularly in the Eastern Church before scripture readings. It has been used in both the Eastern and Western churches on Good Friday since at least 451 (noted in the Acts of the Council of Chalcedon in Asia Minor).

> Holy God,
>
> Holy and mighty,
>
> Holy Immortal One,
>
> have mercy on us.

Preaching

One of the biggest problems related to Good Friday has been the amount of anti-Semitism that has been derived from the Gospel of John and the reproaches that were used during Good Friday beginning in the ninth century. So take care when you preach and speak of the death of Jesus that all of humanity takes blame, rather than any specific group. Focus instead on these words by Brother Alois of Taizé: "The cross is not the last word.... Today we remember that Jesus went to the end of this road: he was betrayed, arrested, sentenced and tortured. He died as the lowest of the low" ("The Cross Is Not the Last Word," http://www.taize.fr/en_arti cle8377.html).

The Passion events have occasionally been put into contemporary language by using words like *torture, noose,* or *electric chair*. Others have suggested that we consider whom we are willing to kill or crucify (see Bill

Kellermann, *Seasons of Faith and Conscience: Kairos, Confession, Liturgy [Seasons]* (Maryknoll, N.Y.: Orbis, 1991, 176–180). For longer services consider telling the story from the point of view of the women at the cross, Pilate, Simon of Cyrene, the disciple John, or Joseph of Arimathea.

Holy Saturday

Prayer for Holy Saturday

God of steadfast love, did you grieve on this day, knowing that we had killed your Son, turned away from his teachings and from your reaching out to us? Did your heart break? *(silence)*

We are truly sorrowful for our part in rejecting Jesus and in rejecting you. Forgive us, forgive us. *(silence)*

Thank you for not taking your love and mercy away from us. Thank you for forgiving us and loving us. Through the crucified Christ, we pray. Amen.

The Easter Vigil

Preparation

In the Easter Vigil the sacraments of baptism and communion celebrate the normal progression of Christian entrance into community. The service itself has a sense of movement that is enhanced by procession—from outside the church building to the sanctuary, from the back of the sanctuary to the front or center, from shadows to light, from the stories of creation up through the story of resurrection, from baptism to communion, from death and sin to life.

The most important symbols for the Vigil are the Paschal, or Easter, candle and the baptismal font, so whatever flowers are included should leave these symbols central and accessible. Many congregations still follow the tradition of the early medieval period of representing a garden for Easter; remember that lilies tend to aggravate allergies and don't last as long as some other varieties, so mix up your garden.

Prepare to give directions to visitors and have all participatory elements clearly explained as needed, with texts in the bulletin or projected on a screen in view of the entire congregation. This is a time to involve many persons as readers for various scriptures (see notes below for choral readings as well), as candle-bearers and lighters, and as instrumentalists. Drawing on the earliest known Eucharistic traditions, some churches follow the Vigil with a breakfast of bread, cheese, milk, honey, and fruit (*Liturgical Year*, 321).

Scriptures

Since these readings are repeated each year, some congregations invite persons to memorize a particular scripture and present it each year. Readers are designated where two or more can be easily used. If a shortened vigil is done, sing "God of the sparrow, God of the whale" by Vajda, which contains many images from the scriptures used.

Old Testament Readings and Psalms (Years A, B, C; * denotes essential readings throughout history)

*Gen. 1:1–2:4a (narrator and God) and **Ps. 136:1-9, 23-26** (response: **For God's steadfast love endures forever**)

Before a Word was said (Kaan); Give thanks for wolf and bird (Damon)

Gen. 7:1-5, 11-18; 8:6-18; 9:8-13; and Ps. 46

I will set my bows in the clouds (Damon); In the midst of new dimensions (Rush)

Gen. 22:1-18 (God, Abraham, Isaac, angel, narrator) and **Ps. 16**

When father Abraham went out (Pratt Green); Saranam, saranam (trad. Pakistani)

*Exod. 14:10-31; 15:20-21 (Moses, narrator, Israelites, Miriam) and **Exod. 15:1b-13, 17-18**

When Israel was in Egypt's land (spiritual); Come, ye faithful, raise the strain/song (John of Damascus); Like Miriam who danced to praise (Keithahn)

43

Isa. 55:1-11 and Isa. 12:2-6

Come, all of you (Laotian); Surely it is God who saves me (White)

Prov. 8:1-8, 19-21; 9:4b-6 and Ps. 19

Come and see the ways of wisdom (Duck); Wake every breath and string (Bringle)

Ezek. 36:24-28 and Pss. 42, 43

Give me a clean heart (Douroux); The thirsty deer longs for the streams (Mulrain)

Ezek. 37:1-14 (Ezekiel, God, narrator) and Ps. 143

Ezekiel cried, "Dem dry bones" (spiritual); O Lord, hear my prayer (Taizé)

Zeph. 3:14-20 and Ps. 98

Gather us in (Haugen); To God compose a song of joy (Duck)

New Testament Readings and Psalm

Romans 6:3-11 and Ps. 114

We know that Christ is raised (Geyer); Lead on, O cloud of Presence (Duck)

*Gospel: **A Matt. 28:1-10; B Mark 16:1-8; C Luke 24:1-12** (parts for various readers in each)

Christ is alive (Wren); Cristo vive/Christ is risen (Martinez); Easter people, raise your voices (James); Woman, weeping in the garden (Damon)

Elements of Worship

Names and Adjectives for God That Are Particularly Appropriate for the Easter Vigil

Creator of all	God our provider
Faithful God	Living God
God of holiness and light	Parent of all who believe in you
God of our salvation	Redeeming God
God of steadfast love	

Hymns, Songs, and Spirituals (See above for things related to specific scriptures and below for baptism and communion.)

For the Vigil, percussion instruments, particularly drums and bells, are appropriate. Some congregations use percussion during the lighting of the candles and procession into the sanctuary, saving the ringing of bells until the proclamation of resurrection. Using an "Alleluia" from another country, region, or tradition (e.g., Caribbean, Honduran, Taizé, Togolese, or Celtic) links the congregation with the world church. Teach the "Alleluia" as people are gathering, and then use it during times of movement into the sanctuary, between scripture readings, to the font, to the table. To connect over time, use the Exsultet (see below) and psalms, which come with centuries of use by the church.

Entrance with light

Christ, whose glory fills the skies (Wesley)

Baptism

At the font we start our journey (Rowthorn)

I'm going on a journey (Larkin and Bonnemere)

O blessed spring (Cherwien)

Remember and rejoice (Duck; for baptismal remembrance)

Wade in the water (spiritual)

Water, River, Spirit, Grace (Troeger)

Communion Hymns and Songs

(Congregations May Sing Easter Hymns)

At dawn, the women made their way (Bringle)

Come, you faithful, raise the strain (John of Damascus)

Coming together for wine and for bread (Tice)

I come with joy (Wren)

In the singing (Murray)

Sing alleluia to the Lord (Stassen)

Te ofrecemos, Padre nuestro (Misa Popular Nicaragüense)

Beginning the Easter Vigil

Some traditions recommend beginning the service with the sanctuary as it ended on Good Friday, with any black drapes in place and with paraments, crosses, flowers, and candlesticks removed. Then during the opening hymn, after the Paschal candle has been brought forth, bring in cross, candlesticks, Easter paraments, flowers, and so forth, to ready the sanctuary for the celebration of resurrection. Other traditions suggest that the sanctuary may be readied earlier, especially in warmer climates where the Vigil may begin outdoors. Smaller congregations may wish to let each member light their candle from the Paschal candle; larger congregations may want to have ushers or acolytes ready to assist in the passing of the light.

The Procession of the Paschal Candle

This could be sung a musical step higher each time to enhance the sense of anticipation. The light may be passed among the congregation first, then processed into church or the opposite: Paschal candle processed into sanctuary and then once there, all candles lit (or only Paschal candle used).

Leader, at the back of the sanctuary: Friends in Christ, behold the light of Christ.

All: Thanks be to God.

Leader, halfway to the altar table: Friends in Christ, behold the light of Christ.

All: Thanks be to God.

Leader, after candle put into place by the altar table: Friends in Christ, behold the light of Christ.

All: Thanks be to God.

Leader: Come, let us worship.

Preaching

Preaching at the Easter Vigil is not the center of the service as it might be at worship on Easter day. For the Vigil, the scripture readings, Paschal candle, and baptisms or renewal of baptism are central. Any preaching should reinforce or give any necessary explanations of the scripture readings, without trying to explain away the mystery of the resurrection and God's reconciliation with us through the cross.

Second Service of Easter/Easter Day

Preparation

If worshiping outdoors, have the congregation (not simply the presenter) face the rising sun. The butterfly and lily have long been used as symbols of Easter—the butterfly, for its resurrection from the cocoon it entered as a caterpillar; and the lily, for its flowering from a "dead" bulb. An older, now less-used symbol is the rooster who announces resurrection and calls the world to live as resurrected.

Visual art might include Paul T. Granlund's cast bronze sculpture "Resurrection II" (originally on the cover of *ARTS Advocate* [UCC Fellowship in the Arts] 12:1 [Winter 1990]) and Henry Ossawa Tanner's "Three Marys" (1910, Fisk University); these two may be found in *IW* 1: 185, 254. Other options include Anton Krajnc's "Resurrection" (1996) fresco in the chapel of Castle Bernau in Austria, and "La resurrection" by Piero della Francesca (ca. 1460; Museo Civico of Sansepolcro).

Scriptures: Resurrection of Jesus Christ/Easter Day/2nd Service of Easter. See Easter hymns under gospel readings for Easter vigil.

A Acts 10:34-43 or Jer. 31:1-6; Ps. 118:1-2, 14-24; Col. 3:1-4 or Acts 10:34-43; John 20:1-18 or Matt. 28:1-10

B Acts 10:34-43 or Isa. 25:6-9; Ps. 118:1-2, 14-24; 1 Cor. 15:1-11 or Acts 10:34-43; John 20:1-18 or Mark 16:1-8

C Acts 10:34-43 or Isa. 65:17-25; Ps. 118:1-2, 14-24; 1 Cor. 15:19-26 or Acts 10:34-43; John 20:1-18 or Luke 24:1-12

Call to Worship or Passing of the Peace of Christ

Friends of Christ, on resurrection day, let us embrace one another in joy, as we forgive everything.

Drama

In medieval times, as the Easter Vigil faded, some churches began doing a short liturgical dialogue-drama, at the first service of Easter. "Visit to the Sepulchre" or "*Quem quaeritis*/Whom do you seek?" involves three women and the angel at the tomb, drawn from Mark's and Luke's accounts of the resurrection (Frank Senn, *The People's Work: A Social History of the Liturgy* [Minneapolis: Fortress, 2006], 165).

Refrain from the Exsultet, traced back at least to the seventh century in Gaul, and sung only on Easter

> Exalt, all creation, around God's throne!
>
> Jesus Christ, our Savior, is risen!
>
> Sound the trumpet of salvation!
>
> Rejoice, heavenly powers!
>
> Sing, choirs of angels!
>
> Jesus Christ, our Savior, is risen!

Prayer Response

God of life and hope, raise us with Christ.

Ancient Sending

Go and tell the world that Jesus is alive. He goes before you into the streets and your homes, offices, and markets, prisons and hospitals. Look, and you will see him (John Chrysostom).

Preaching

The story itself is full of power, whether the gospel or Peter's summary in Acts 10:34-43. Name the resurrection stories of your congregation, your neighborhood, the world. Look at the story from various perspectives: Peter, Mary Magdalene, Mary the mother of Jesus, the centurion at the tomb, Cleopas on the road to Emmaus. Resurrection is a liberative action: in what tombs are we and others around us living? The "old Jesus" is not here—the new Jesus is. What old pieces of ourselves need to be lost to make room for our resurrected, Christlike selves?

For additional inspiration for preaching, see the following poems and readings: "Easter" by Gerard Manley Hopkins (1866; public domain); and "Easter" by George Herbert (in *The Temple* [1633]); "Song on the Road to Emmaus" by Dorothea Sölle in *Revolutionary Patience* (New York: Orbis, 1984, 46–48); "The Three Women: Easter Script 1," in *Stages on the Way* (Chicago: Iona Community/GIA, 2000 , 190–192); and "Noli me tangere (Fresco: Fra Angelico)" by Jean Janzen in *Christian Century* 115:11 (April 8, 1998): 368.

Great Fifty Days: Alleluia! Christ Is Risen!

Preparation

These are fifty days for the church to practice living resurrection. The Paschal candle, lit during the Easter Vigil or the first service of Easter, remains by the altar table until the celebration of the Ascension. Festive processions, banners, light, white and gold, standing for prayer—are all appropriate during this season. If your congregation does not celebrate communion weekly, this is a particularly appropriate time to do so; as the risen Christ feasted with his early disciples (after the walk to Emmaus and at breakfast on the beach), so communion is a strong reminder of the presence of the risen Christ among us.

Visual art for this season might include the contemporary pieces: "Hallelujah" (1969) by Osmond Watson, "Liberation" by Frederick Horsman Varley (1881–1969), and "Disciples Healing the Sick" (ca. 1930) by Henry Ossawa Tanner (*IW* 3:201, 202, 253).

Some ideas for capturing and releasing some of God's resurrection power in worship this season:

Add instruments of all sizes and shapes from trumpets to children's percussion instruments.

Sing more together.

Allow for movement within worship.

Reaffirm everyone's baptism, with testimony and joy.

Build up the beloved community, following the example of the early church (Acts).

Scriptures for the Great Fifty Days, the Sundays of Easter (Ascension noted separately), along with Hymns, Songs, and Spirituals

Year A

• 2nd Sunday: Acts 2:14a, 22-32; Ps. 16; 1 Pet. 1:3-9; John 20:19-31 "Peace be with you!"; Bless the Lord, my soul (Taizé)

• 3rd Sunday: Acts 2:14a, 36-41; Ps. 116:1-4, 12-19; 1 Pet. 1:17-23; Luke 24:13-35; Holy Presence, Holy Teacher (Murray); O thou who this mysterious bread (Wesley)

• 4th Sunday: Acts 2:42-47; Ps. 23; 1 Pet. 2:19-25; John 10:1-10; When at this table (Murray); God walks with us (a contemporary version of "He leadeth me") (Aldredge-Clanton)

• 5th Sunday: Acts 7:55-60; Ps. 31:1-5, 15-16; 1 Pet. 2:2-10; John 14:1-14; Peace, be not anxious (Bringle); His Eye Is on the Sparrow (Martin)

• 6th Sunday: Acts 17:22-31; Ps. 66:8-20; 1 Pet. 3:13-22; John 14:15-21; Lord, I want to be more loving (spiritual); The love of God receives us (Damon)

• 7th Sunday of Easter, if Ascension not observed here: Acts 1:6-14; Ps. 68:1-10, 32-35; 1 Pet. 4:12-14; 5:6-11; John 17:1-11; Come now, O Prince of Peace (Lee); Unidos/Together (Villanueva); Jesus is the center (Damon)

Year B

• 2nd Sunday: Acts 4:32-35; Ps. 133; 1 John 1:1–2:2; John 20:19-31; How good is it (Duck); We are not our own (Wren)

• 3rd Sunday: Acts 3:12-19; Ps. 4; 1 John 3:1-7; Luke 24:36b-48; O sons and daughters, let us sing (Tisserand); Cristo vive/Christ is risen (Martinez)

• 4th Sunday: Acts 4:5-12; Ps. 23; 1 John 3:16-24; John 10:11-18; Love one another (Chepponis); You, Lord, are both Lamb and Shepherd (Dunstan)

• 5th Sunday: Acts 8:26-40; Ps. 22:25-31; 1 John 4:7-21; John 15:1-8; Abide in me (Wise); O blessed spring (Cherwien)

• 6th Sunday: Acts 10:44-48; Ps. 98; 1 John 5:1-6; John 15:9-17; Your love, O God (Frostenson); Jesu, Jesu, fill us with your love (Colvin)

• 7th Sunday, if Ascension not observed here: Acts 1:15-17, 21-26; Ps. 1; 1 John 5:9-13; John 17:6-19; Lord, I want to be more holy (spiritual); We shall not be moved (spiritual)

Year C

• 2nd Sunday: Acts 5:27-32; Ps. 118:14-29 or Psalm 150; Rev. 1:4-8; John 20:19-31; Cristo vive/Christ is risen (Martinez); "Peace be with you!" Jesus said (Tice)

• 3rd Sunday: Acts 9:1-6 (7-20); Ps. 30; Rev. 5:11-14; John 21:1-19; Christ the Lord has risen (Colvin); This is a day of new beginnings (Wren)

• 4th Sunday: Acts 9:36-43; Ps. 23; Rev. 7:9-17; John 10:22-30; Praise ye the Lord (Cleveland); O Holy Spirit, Root of life (Janzen on Hildegard of Bingen)

• 5th Sunday: Acts 11:1-18; Ps. 148; Rev. 21:1-6; John 13:31-35; Spirit of the living God (Iverson); There'll be joy in the morning (Sleeth)

• 6th Sunday: Acts 16:9-15; Ps. 67; Rev. 21:10, 22–22:5; John 14:23-29 or John 5:1-9; Wade in the water (spiritual); Sent out in Jesus' name (anon.)

• 7th Sunday, if Ascension not observed here: Acts 16:16-34; Ps. 97; Rev. 22:12-14, 16-17, 20-21; John 17:20-26; Righteous and holy (Paris); Make your prayer and music one (Troeger)

Elements of Worship

Names and Adjectives Particularly Appropriate for God in This Season

Brightness of God's glory	God of resurrection power
Christ, the tree of life	Great and loving God
Fount of justice	Heartbeat of our world
Glorious Source of life	Life-giving God
God of life	Risen Christ
God of mystery	Worker of wonders
God of never-ending hope	

Call to Worship: Alleluia, Christ is risen! **Christ is risen indeed, alleluia!**

(Note that in congregational prayers in this book, often the first line is said by the leader to ease the beginning-together of the prayer.)

General Prayer for the Great Fifty Days

We sing of your love, **O God who gives us love.**

We sing of your peace, **O God who gives us peace.**

We sing of your joy, **O God who gives us joy.**

We sing of your beauty, **O God who makes us beautiful.**

We sing of your Word, **O God who gives us voice.**

We pray that others will hear our song and know that you are real.

Amen. (Michele Lynne Holloway)

Preaching

We are so accustomed to the Easter story that it seldom shakes us up. But think of those who were shaken: the women who went to the tomb; Peter and John, who ran there following Mary's amazing story; Thomas, who proclaimed, "My Lord and my God!"; the nascent church, called from hiding to public works empowered by the Holy Spirit, gathering, telling the story, baptizing, beginning a new type of life together that will become church. For all those who knew and believed in Jesus and then in his resurrection, life was turned upside down and inside out. If even crucifixion is not the last word, if a shattered body can rise again to offer peace and talk with disciples, if multitudes can seek baptism upon hearing the Word of God and seeing the Spirit at work, God has much more yet in store for us!

This season also challenges the powers that be in society and institutions, reminding us daily, as the early church discovered, that God is in charge, not human beings. Since we know God is in charge, where do we see resurrection: in ourselves, in our church, in our world? For additional inspiration for preaching, see "Sermons for Eastertide," by Thomas H. Troeger in *Circuit Rider* (March 1994, 18–19).

All that we need has already been given to us—grace abundant and overflowing. In these Great Fifty Days, let this message of God's amazing power and exuberant love for the world be preached and praised in our churches.

Ascension

Preparation

This fortieth day of Easter celebrates the Ascension of Jesus Christ into heaven (Acts 1:6-11). The color for Ascension, like all of the Great Fifty Days, is white. The Paschal candle has central place by the altar table; by the next service it will be moved to the baptismal font. Since this service actually occurs on a Thursday, it is a good occasion for a church supper followed by a worship service, or a worship service before any usual Thursday evening activities such as choir rehearsal or meetings. For those churches who do not celebrate Ascension on Thursday, it is appropriate to celebrate on the seventh Sunday of Easter. Visual art suggestions include the Ascension window, with Christ holding the world, by Brother Eric from the Church of the Resurrection at Taizé (available online at http://www.taize.fr/en_article8552.html); the Eastern Orthodox icon of Jesus the Pantocrator ("Ruler of All"); and the Mount of Olives, the site traditionally associated with the Ascension.

Scriptures

A, B, C: Acts 1:1-11; Ps. 47 or Ps. 93; Eph. 1:15-23; Luke 24:44-53

Elements of Worship

Names and Adjectives for God Particularly Appropriate for This Day

Christ, Glory of Glories	Fullness of Glory, Fullness of Love
Christ of all times and places	God of the universe
Everlasting Peace	

Litany of Thanksgiving for the Ascension
Response: O God, we give you thanks and glory.

For the Word came from you and has returned to you,   **R**

For restoring the full glory of Jesus Christ,   **R**

For holding our human experience in your heart,   **R**

For raising up the entire fallen creation,   **R**

For the freedom of the Risen One from confines of time and space,   **R**

For the promise of your Holy Spirit,   **R**

(may be followed by a Gloria, Doxology, or the fifth/final stanza of Brian Wren's "Christ Is Alive")

Doxology for Ascension (to be sung to OLD 100TH or TRURO or GIFT OF LOVE)

> Praise God, who holds us in God's heart,
> Praise Christ, who never will depart,
> > Praise Spirit, who will ever come,
> Praise Trinity, who is our home.

Hymns, Songs, and Spirituals

Christ is alive, and the universe must celebrate (Murray)

Christ is alive! Let Christians sing (Wren)

God of futures yet unfolding (Bringle)

Hail the day that sees him rise (Wesley)

Hail thee, festival day (Ascension verse) (Fortunatus)

Jesus is the center (Damon)

Shout to the Lord (Zschech)

Preaching

The theology connected with Christ's Ascension is particularly important to some strands of Christianity, who interpret it as the keeping of Christ's humanity by God and the clear moment when Christ takes his place with the Creator in order to rule all creation. For others, ascension is the enlargement of access to Christ's divinity by people in all times and all places. Through the Ascension we are as close to Jesus wherever we are on the globe as were his disciples back in Galilee in the first century (Stookey, *Calendar*, 71). Rather than focus on the confusing scientific "hows" of Ascension, give thanks for its "why" for our lives (see litany above).

Pentecost

Preparation

This day celebrates the descent of the Holy Spirit on the followers of Jesus gathered in Jerusalem, which emboldened them to preach the good news and empowered their ministry. Pentecost has many visual symbols that can be used, so decide your theme and focus, perhaps rotating each year:

• Energizing and purifying fire of the Holy Spirit: flames, tongues of fire, red clothes, red ribbons on ends of pews, geraniums and poinsettias (in the Southern Hemisphere these are just coming into bloom, see Carmen Pilcher, "Poinsettia: Christmas or Pentecost—Celebrating Liturgy in the Great South Land That Is Australia" in *Worship,* 81:6 [November 2007])

• Winds of change and hope of the Holy Spirit: kite, wind chimes, wind socks, pinwheels, streamers, fans

• Peace and wisdom of the Holy Spirit: doves, red candles, times of silence

• The founding of the church and empowering of its members: rocks (Matt. 16:18), birthday cake, red/yellow/orange stoles for everyone (all ages) made from crepe paper for everyone, since we are all ministers (Lynne Davis Vandercook, "Children and the Liturgical Year: Reflections on Practical Application," in *Reformed Liturgy and Music* [Winter 1992]: 23–25).

The Easter/Great Fifty Days colors of white (Christ and baptism) and gold (stress its flame-like tones) continue, with the addition of red for this day. "And It Filled All the House" by Anna Raimondi is an energetic Hawaiian banner depicting the descent of the Holy Spirit (*IW* 3:199).

Scripture

(Note that the first and second readings are the same in each cycle.)
A Acts 2:1-21; Ps. 104:24-34, 35b; 1 Cor. 12:3b-13 or Acts 2:1-21; John 20:19-23 or 7:37-39

B Acts 2:1-21; Ps. 104:24-34, 35b; Rom. 8:22-27 or Acts 2:1-21; John 15:26-27; 16:4b-15

C Acts 2:1-21; Ps. 104:24-34, 35b; Rom. 8:14-17 or Acts 2:1-21; John 14:8-17, (25-27)

Elements of Worship

Names and Adjectives for God That Are Particularly Appropriate on This Day and in the Season Following

Birthing Spirit	Presence Divine
Breath Divine	Promise of God
Burning Spirit	Radiant Life
Comforter	Restorer of our right minds
Connecting Spirit	Revealing Spirit
Consuming Fire	Root of all being
Energizing Spirit	Spirit of counsel
Eternal Spark	Spirit of everlasting grace
Eternal Spirit	Spirit of goodness and truth
Everlasting Home	Spirit of pure and holy love
Fire of the Spirit	Spirit of righteousness
God of the Winds	Spirit of sanctifying grace
Holy Fire	Spirit of wisdom
Indwelling God	Spirit, the Giver of life
Light of clarity	Truth-telling Spirit
Paraclete	

Call to Worship

Greetings in different languages (such as peace [*paz, paix, shalom, salaam, Vrede, Friede, Uxolo, Mír, héping*] or love [*amor, agape, filios, die Liebe, amour, kärlek*]) and also Acts 2:4 and/or Lord's Prayer in different languages

Prayer Response

Holy Spirit, open the door of faith and grace to us.

Collects

Divine spark,

the source of all creation,

bring your power into our lives,

and light our journeys of discovery

that we may always be illuminated by your grace. (Cordelia Burpee)

Hymns, Songs, and Spirituals (Acts 2)

Percussion: cymbals rolled and crashed, tympani; contemporary music

As a fire is meant for burning (Duck)

Come, O Holy Spirit, come/Wa wa wa Emimimo (Yoruba)

Holy Spirit, come to us (Taizé)

I'm gonna sing when the Spirit says sing (spiritual)

Like the murmur of the dove's song (Daw)

The Pentecostal fire that flashed (Bringle)

The Spirit is a dove (Tice)

This holy covenant was made (Dunstan)

Through our fragmentary prayers (Troeger)

Preaching

We enter now into the season of boldness, like the apostles, no longer in hiding, but proclaiming the good news of Jesus Christ through our actions wherever we go. (For inspiration and challenges, see Kellermann, *Seasons*, 199–206.) Remember that the purposes of the tongues of fire were to glorify God, to announce the presence of the Holy Spirit, and to promote reconciliation among people of various places and languages.

ASH WEDNESDAY

Preparation

This day is the beginning of our Lenten journey. For congregations who are unaccustomed to **signation** (signing) with ashes, words of repentance might be written on index cards and then burned in a wok, then words of assurance proclaimed. Some churches do this as a first step, then move toward receiving ashes another year.

The service for Ash Wednesday has traditionally included Psalm 51, prayers of confession and the sign of ashes, often in the shape of the cross. In some churches this is also a fast day. The ashes may be made from the dried palm branches of the previous year, signifying that enthusiasm which has become brittle and dry over the year; ashes may also be purchased through Christian supply stores. It is not necessary to add anything to the ashes, as it is not the mark that is important (cf. Matt. 6:16-18) but the action of our desire to repent. Wood (or paper) ashes are not acceptable for use in signation as when mixed with water they are alkaline, which may burn the skin.

The traditional color for Ash Wednesday, as the first day of Lent, is purple, but some churches use gray or black instead or as a second color. Rough fabrics, such as sackcloth, rather than smooth are appropriate.

Scriptures

A, B, C: Joel 2:1-2, 12-17 or Isa. 58:1-12; Ps. 51:1-17; 2 Cor. 5:20b–6:10; Matt. 6:1-6, 16-21

Order of Service

Prelude or silent processional of worship leaders

Call to Worship

One: This is a day of God's mercy. We are mortal, we sin, and we will die.

Many: We need God and God's extravagant grace.

Hymns, Songs, and Spirituals

This is a day for singing "Kyrie/God, have mercy"; in one of its many musical settings: Byzantine chant, Russian Orthodox liturgy, the Guarani people of Paraguay, Taizé, Ghana's Dinah Reindorf, Iona's John Bell, Canada's Healey Willan and William S. Kervin, Swee Hong Lim of Singapore.

> Dust and ashes touch our face (Wren)
>
> Forgive us, Lord/Perdón, Dios (Lockward)
>
> Give me a clean heart (Douroux)
>
> O for a heart to praise my God (Wesley)
>
> Sunday's palms are Wednesday's ashes (Whitney)

Psalm 51

Time for Silent Repentance

Receiving ashes: Persons come forward, as they are able, to receive the ashes from the pastor or worship leader. Ashes are usually held in a small bowl. Ashes may be signed on the back of the hand or the forehead, with one of the following phrases:

> Turn around, and believe the gospel.
>
> Repent and believe the good news: God forgives us and loves us.
>
> You are dust, and to dust you shall return (Gen. 3:19)
>
> Ashes to ashes, dust to dust. Remember that you are mortal.
>
> Receive these ashes, knowing that God hears your confession and forgives your sin.

Some churches celebrate **communion** after receiving the ashes, as a sign of God's acceptance of our repentance and forgiveness; in these churches coming to receive ashes and to receive communion would be separate events (not just one). Other churches let ashes and confession be the primary symbols for the service.

Preaching

Preaching may draw from these images, but let confession and ashes be the primary symbol:

- our mortality and finiteness, God's infinity and promises
- ashes not only for our own personal sin, but the sins of humanity, especially those where ashes were involved: Bergen-Belsen, Auschwitz, Hiroshima, Nagasaki, Bosnia, Iraq, the Twin Towers of New York City
- the ashes of our hopes and dreams that need to be exchanged for the hopes and dreams of God
- rather than giving up, taking on: practicing regular devotion, volunteering, praying for enemies, giving to those less fortunate, performing daily kind deeds

Lent: A Long Period of Grace, Cyril of Jerusalem (ca. 315–386)

Preparation

Lent has a tradition of being a somber time in the church, with desert sands and wilderness, rough fabrics, purples and grays, no alleluias. Yet the journey in the wilderness leads Jesus to Jerusalem, to a cross and to a tomb, both appropriate symbols for this season. So, too, our journey has a goal, fresh baptismal waters (keep the font visible) and living into the realities of the cross and resurrection in our lives and in our world. Some congregations don't have flowers or greenery in the sanctuary during Lent; other congregations might have a blooming cactus or bulbs beginning to sprout. Other symbols of the season include sackcloth, ashes, rocks, thorns, or a bare tree. Empty spaces are also important during Lent, space for prayer and for God.

Scriptures in Lent; Hymns, Songs, and Scriptures

(see also general music below in Hymns, Songs, and Spirituals)

Year A

• 1st Sunday: Gen. 2:15-17; 3:1-7; Ps. 32; Rom. 5:12-19; Matt. 4:1-11; Jesus, tempted in the desert (Stuempfle); Lord, who throughout these forty days (Hernaman)

• 2nd Sunday: Gen. 12:1-4a; Ps. 121; Rom. 4:1-5, 13-17; John 3:1-17 or Matt. 17:1-9; We are God's people (Leech); I lift my eyes to the hills (Andrus)

• 3rd Sunday: Exod. 17:1-7; Ps. 95; Rom. 5:1-11; John 4:5-42; I AM the living water (Tice); Woman in the night (verse 4, Woman at the well) (Wren)

• 4th Sunday: 1 Sam. 16:1-13; Ps. 23; Eph. 5:8-14; John 9:1-41; Eat this bread and never hunger (Damon); You, Lord, are both Lamb and Shepherd (Dunstan)

• 5th Sunday: Ezek. 37:1-14; Ps. 130; Rom. 8:6-11; John 11:1-45; Eat this bread and never hunger (Damon); Ezekiel connected those dry bones (spiritual)

Year B

• 1st Sunday: Gen. 9:8-17; Ps. 25:1-10; 1 Pet. 3:18-22; Mark 1:9-15; Wild and lone the prophet's voice (Daw); I will set my bows in the clouds (Damon)

• 2nd Sunday: Gen. 17:1-7, 15-16; Ps. 22:23-31; Rom. 4:13-25; Mark 8:31-38 or Mark 9:2-9; Two fishermen (verses 3 and 4) (Toolan); I will set my bows in the clouds (Damon)

• 3rd Sunday: Exod. 20:1-17; Ps. 19; 1 Cor. 1:18-25; John 2:13-22; Give me a clean heart (Douroux); The cross on the hill is the measuring rod (Troeger)

• 4th Sunday: Num. 21:4-9; Ps. 107:1-3, 17-22; Eph. 2:1-10; John 3:14-21; Grace alone (Brown and Nelson); I will set my bows in the clouds (Damon)

• 5th Sunday: Jer. 31:31-34; Ps. 51:1-12 or Ps. 119:9-16; Heb. 5:5-10; John 12:20-33; Forgive us, Lord/Perdón, Dios (Lockward); I will set my bows in the clouds (Damon)

Year C

• 1st Sunday: Deut. 26:1-11; Ps. 91:1-2, 9-16; Rom. 10:8b-13; Luke 4:1-13; Jesus walked this lonesome valley (spiritual); On eagles' wings (Joncas)

• 2nd Sunday: Gen. 15:1-12, 17-18; Ps. 27; Phil. 3:17–4:1; Luke 13:31-35 or Luke 9:28-36, (37-43); Lord, who throughout these forty days (Hernaman); The Lord is my light (Taizé)

• 3rd Sunday: Isa. 55:1-9; Ps. 63:1-8; 1 Cor. 10:1-13; Luke 13:1-9; Give me a clean heart (Douroux); Come, all of you (Laotian)

• 4th Sunday: Josh. 5:9-12; Ps. 32; 2 Cor. 5:16-21; Luke 15:1-3, 11b-32; God's great love is so amazing (Gillette); prayer below; Saranam, saranam (trad. Pakistani)

• 5th Sunday: Isa. 43:16-21; Ps. 126; Phil. 3:4b-14; John 12:1-8; A woman poured her jar of rich perfume (Tice); refrain of We shall come rejoicing, bringing in the sheaves (Shaw); Ask ye what great thing I know (Schwedler)

Elements of Worship

Names and Adjectives for God Particularly Appropriate in This Season

Christ, Crucified One	God of the wilderness
Christ, the Suffering Servant	God, our Life-Giver
Christ, the Way	God, rich in mercy
Compassionate God	God who keeps promises
Covenant God	God who sets a table in the
Dreamer of new worlds	wilderness
God in our terror, God in	One who weeps with us
our calm	Searcher of hearts
God of all consolation	Spirit of living water
God of justice	Spirit of mercy

God of mercy	Spirit of wind, sand, and fire
God of our forebears	Steadfast God
God of the exodus	Strong Rock

Call to Worship (for use every week in Lent)

One: God has called us to this holy place.

Many: We are travelers on a journey of faith.

One: In this season of Lent, we journey in the shadow of the cross and the light of baptismal waters.

Many: We seek to learn more of Jesus, who reconciles us to God and to one another.

One: Let us enter into this time of worship with open hearts and minds.

Collect

God of change, **who created cycles of life and death and growing, transform us this Lent, grow in us;**

let die in us bad habits and mean thoughts,

bring to life in us the loving and challenging spirit of Jesus,

that we might take part more deeply in your promises and vision for creation.

Through your Spirit that sustains us in all changes, we pray. Amen.

Hymns, Songs, and Spirituals, General—See above for Specific Pieces for Scriptures

Jesus walked this lonesome valley (spiritual)

When we are tested and wrestle alone (Duck)

Confessions

Many churches who do not regularly use confessions add them into their Lenten services. Other congregations who do confession regularly add the reminders from scripture about what defines righteous living, such as the Ten Commandments, Exod. 20:1-17; Micah 6:8; or the Great Commandment, Matt. 22:37-40.

1. Jesus Christ knows our temptations and feels our urges to take the easy way rather than the hard paths of discipleship. Yet Jesus comes to announce to us God's grace and mercy before we can even ask. Come, let us confess together the times we have not done the will of God as we sing the church's ancient cry of "God, have mercy": sing a *Kyrie* (e.g., that from the Russian Orthodox liturgy or Taizé or the Byzantine chant) then pause for silence, announce again God's forgiving love, and then sing something like "Move me to do your will" by Henderson or "Mayenziwe/Your will be done on earth" (South African) or "The kingdom of God is justice and peace" (Taizé).

2. *With silences between*

Good Judge, pardon us.

Good Shepherd, have mercy on us.

Good Savior, deliver us.

Words of Assurance: Our Good Shepherd has given his life for us sheep, to assure us that we are forgiven. Be at peace.

3. *With silences or witness (adapted from James 4:8)*

The writer to James says, "Cleanse your hands, you sinners." What sins have clung to our hands, to your hands, this week?

The writer to James continues, "Purify your hearts, you backsliders" (*paraphrased*). What has soiled your hearts this week? What is soiling the heart of the world that we have a part in and need to confess?

Witnessing to the assurance of pardon

Invite the congregation to witness by completing the sentence "Forgiveness is...."

4. We have failed...

We have disappointed you, O God...

We have stepped back when you called us forward...

We have despaired instead of grasping onto your hope ...

We have pretended that we did not need you or others ...

We have forgotten that we are your people ...

Words of Assurance: God is full of grace and mercy. Know this, and re-member whose you are.

Litany, *with response from John 1:16*

Response: From your fullness we have all received, grace upon grace.

Jesus, fount of life and holiness,   **R**

Jesus, teacher and feeder of the hungry,   **R**

Jesus, healer of the sick,   **R**

Jesus, sign of the new covenant,   **R**

Jesus, follower of God's will to the end,   **R**

Jesus, Lamb of God,   **R**

Jesus, redeemer of the world,   **R**

Prayer, Luke 15:11-32, Year C, Fourth Sunday in Lent

    Eternal father, loving mother, holy parent,

    who knows and loves us from our first stirrings,

    watch over our children,

  the wandering and the lost,

  the confused and the hiding,

  the bold and the foolhardy,

    hold them in your gentle embrace,

    turn them toward their path

    that they may find their hearts' desire and know that it is you.

    Amen. (Cordelia Burpee)

Preaching

Lent is a season of being turned around by God, in Greek, *metanoia*. Sometimes this is a total change in direction, or 180-degree change; other times it is movement in small increments, as tacking a sailboat to correct our course to better match God's wind. Every day we have opportunities for *metanoia*—are we taking them?

What wilderness is your community wandering through? Lent is sometimes called "a journey to the edge" . . . of what for your congregation, spiritually, mentally, emotionally, physically?

For further inspiration, see the poem by Jean Janzen, "Instructions: 'For Lent'" in *Paper House* (Intercourse, Pa.: Good Books, 2008).

Palm/Passion Sunday

Preparation

This service begins with a procession celebrating Jesus' triumphal entry into Jerusalem and ends with his trial, crucifixion, and burial. It is a multisensory day, so involve as many people as possible in planning and leading the procession, in obtaining ecologically raised palms or other local branches, in leading the litany or singing during the procession or playing rhythm instruments or handbells, and in voicing the Passion story. Some congregations, who are trying to work with or have an impact on their neighborhoods, take their palm procession to the streets. Have something simple to sing or chant on the way and perhaps provide a handout of service times through Easter and outreach activities of the church for observers. The color for this day varies: from red for palms and purple for the Passion story; from purple for the royalty of the procession and red for the blood of the Passion; to red or purple for the palm procession and grays and blacks for the Passion. Pay attention to mobility issues so that all may participate joyfully in the procession; this day is a good time to practice working together so that everyone may take part.

Scriptures

Note that Psalms 118:1-2, 19-29; and 31:9-16; Isaiah 50:4-9a; and Philippians 2:5-11 appear each of the three years; only the gospel readings change; alternative gospel Passion readings are long or short versions.

A: Matt. 21:1-11; Matt. 26:14–27:66 or Matt. 27:11-54

B: Mark 11:1-11 or John 12:12-16; Mark 14:1–15:47 or Mark 15:1-39, (40-47)

C: Luke 19:28-40; Luke 22:14–23:56 or Luke 23:1-49

Worship Elements

Names for God Particularly Appropriate for This Day

Humble Jesus   Tried and tested Jesus

Savior   Welcomed Hero

Son of David

Hymns, Songs, and Spirituals

All Glory, laud, and honor (Theodulf), used for centuries for processionals on this day

Hosanna (various settings)

Thanks be to God, our great salvation (Psalm 118) (Duck)

We sang our glad hosannas (Keithahn), (transition palms to Passion)

Were you there? (spiritual)

"Why has God forsaken me?" (Wallace)

Confession

Welcomed Hero, Jesus Christ, teach us the deeper meaning of Hosanna—Save us!

We have forgotten how much we need you, and yet we are floundering by ourselves.

Our world needs your example of leadership and heroism.

Conquering Leader, Innocent Man, Jesus under trial,

let us learn again from you that the way to God is not the way of the world.

Words of Assurance

God said, "This is my beloved Son, listen to him."

In our listening we hear Christ's voice, "Forgive them," and we know ourselves forgiven and freed.

Litany, which might also be used in the Palm Procession

All who know your healing touch shout, "Hosanna!"

All those children you have blessed shout, "Hosanna!"

All those who sensed your love shout, "Hosanna!"

All those who saw Lazarus come out of the tomb shout, "Hosanna!"

All the neighbors of the woman at the well shout, "Hosanna!"

All those who heard your parables about God's coming reign shout, "Hosanna!"

Preaching

The world has always hungered for heroes. This day sets the tone for how Jesus fulfills this role in an unlikely way, entering Jerusalem on a humble donkey, and within days being tried, beaten, and killed as a criminal. Give each gospel story its own perspective, rather than trying to harmonize them. This is one of those days that is so rich in symbolism that keeping silence together in the midst of the readings can be very meaningful.

CHAPTER 3

THE INCARNATION CYCLE

THE TWELVE DAYS OF CHRISTMAS AND EPIPHANY, ADVENT

INTRODUCTION

Missio Dei, Christmas through Epiphany

Writing about Christmas, Brother Alois of Taizé says, "God comes in Jesus to ask everyone, generation after generation, to participate in the work of reconciliation" (http://www.taize.fr/en_article7931.html). Augustine wrote for these days: "Begin, then, to love your neighbor. Break your bread to feed the hungry, and bring into your home the homeless poor; if you see someone naked, clothe him, and do not look down on your own flesh and blood.... In loving and caring for your neighbor you are on a journey" (Mary Ann Simcoe, ed., *A Christmas Sourcebook* [Chicago: Liturgy Training, 1984], 75). In this season of receiving God's most precious gift, are we giving gifts to those who really need our gifts—food for mothers and newborns around the world, partnership with those less fortunate, sharing of wisdom around ways to live rather than ways to die?

Blessing: Rejoice! The gift God gives us in Jesus Christ is love and grace beyond measure; it is abundant and overflows our lives. Children of God, know that you are blessed!

Sending: Go forth through the power of the Holy Spirit,

shining in holiness,

to carry God's overflowing gifts to the world:

food for the hungry, warm clothes for the naked,

shelter for the homeless, love instead of conflict,

and good news about living for all the world!

Missio Dei, Advent

Several early church fathers state the concerns of Advent in challenging ways: Ambrose (ca. 339–397, bishop of Milan) says, "There is your sister or brother, naked, crying! And you stand confused over the choice of an attractive floor covering." Basil (ca. 330–379, Cappadocia) says, "What keeps you from giving now? Isn't the poor person there? Aren't your own warehouses full?...The bread in your cupboard belongs to the hungry person; the coat hanging unused in your closet belongs to the person who needs it" (both quotes found in *An Advent Sourcebook*, ed. Thomas J. O'Gorman [Chicago: Liturgy Training, 1988], 45). Congregations have met these challenges during Advent with baby showers for needy babies in the community, alternative Christmas markets with fair-trade items, offerings to Heifer International or UNICEF, mitten trees in colder climates, books for children, toiletries for persons in homeless shelters, and taking a pledge to give our gifts and presents to those in the world who need them most. How can Advent worship shape us so that these projects are natural and a joyous response to God's love in our lives?

Blessing: May God, who has been present with us

from the beginning of time,

and God, for whom we are waiting, bless us

as we live into the tension of God's vision, here and not yet.

Sending: Let us live by justice and by mercy,

as we wait with hope for Jesus to come.

THE TWELVE DAYS OF CHRISTMAS AND EPIPHANY

Christmas

Preparation

Congregations who have waited through Advent may now set up and bless a Chrismon tree or crèche. Some change the Advent wreath candles to all white, while others add the Christ candle to the wreath. Paraments and stoles should be white and gold, of fine fabrics.

Some congregations feature children's pageants on Christmas Eve or morning, though this can make an already overwhelming time even more so for children. If you do something, keep it simple and scriptural.

Because you may have a large number of visitors, remember to include texts in the bulletin for the Lord's Prayer, any sung responses, and other participatory elements. Have plenty of ushers and greeters on hand. Carolers or handbell ringers on the front walk or in the narthex can also be welcoming.

The Christmas rose, a white rose that blooms in winter, representing the purity of Mary and the child Jesus, is a tradition older than poinsettias, which have been used since the sixteenth century in Mexico, and in the United States since 1828.

Susan Jeffers's painting for "Silent Night" (1984) and Henry Ossawa Tanner's "Angels Appearing before the Shepherds" (ca. 1910) portray the amazing size of angels compared to the smallness of the shepherds, and can help capture some of the awe of this event. Renaissance art includes "The Nativity" by Gerard David (1460–1523), Hugo van der Goes's "Portinari Altarpiece" ca. 1475, or "The Mystical Nativity" by Sandro Botticelli (1445–1510). Contemporary images include "We Saw His Glory" by Iris Hahs-Hoffstetter (*IW*, 3:107; originally in Hans-Ruedi Weber, *Immanuel: The Coming of Jesus in Art and the Bible* [Grand Rapids: Eerdmans; Geneva: World Council of Churches, 1984]).

Elements of Worship

Names and Adjectives Particularly Appropriate for God
on This Day and Season

Astonishing Grace	Mary's son
Brightness of God	Mercy Divine
Brother of the poor	Mother of the Universe
Child of Bethlehem	Pattern of Holiness
Child of joy and peace	Prince of Peace
Christ of hope	Protector of the poor
Christ, Visible Image of Godself	Radiant Child
Christmas God	Redeemer of all
Door of joy	Reflection of God's glory
Dreamer of dreams	Shepherd of the stars
Emmanuel	Son of the living God
Eternal Salvation	Source of Life
Gift of Love	Sun of Justice
Gift of Peace	Surprising Moment of Grace
God of grace and truth	Treasure of the faithful
God who labors	True Love
Great Mystery	Very God of Very God
Heaven-born Child	Welcome Jesus
Inexhaustible Wisdom	Wonderful Counselor
Light that shines in our darkness	Word Made Flesh
Loving Word of God	

Calls to Worship

1. Let us welcome the Christ-Light!

2. Good news, good news! Peace and love!

   ¡Noticias buenas! ¡Paz y amor!

3. Adapted from tradition

One: Tonight/Today Christ the Messiah is born.

All: With all creation we sing, "Glory!"

One: Tonight/Today our Savior has appeared.

All: With all creation we sing, "Glory!"

One: Tonight/Today heaven and earth praise God together.

All: With all creation we sing, "Glory!"

One: Tonight/Today Christ dwells on earth.

All: With all creation we sing, "Glory! Alleluia!"

Collect, adapted from Bede, early British priest and church historian

Christ, our Morning Star, **when the night of this world is past,**

> **give to us your saints the promise of the Light of life,**
>
> > **and open everlasting day,**
>
> **that we might rejoice with all the stars in heaven**
>
> > **and all your creation on earth**
>
> **and become bearers of your light in the world.**
>
> **We pray in your name, Holy Trinity, One God,**
>
> > **now and forever. Amen.**

Doxologies

1. For Christmas Eve, sung to the tune CHRISTMAS, "While shepherds watched their flocks by night," using this traditional English carol text (repeat the fourth line) or ANTIOCH, "Joy to the World" (adding the contemporary lines in parentheses):

> Now let good Christians all begin
>
> a holier life to live,
>
> > and to rejoice and merry be,
>
> for this is Christmas Eve.

(Our God has come to earth

to enflesh a holy life

and show us love.)

2. An ancient doxological stanza, written by Prudentius (348–ca. 413, Latin hymn-writer) with a note by its translator, John Mason Neale (1851), "evening hymn from the Nativity till Epiphany." Sing to DIVINUM MYSTERIUM, "Of the Father's love/heart begotten."

Let the heights of heaven adore Christ,

angel hosts, with praises sing!

Powers, dominions, bow before the babe,

praises to our God and Christ bring.

Let no tongue on earth be silent,

every voice in concert ring

evermore and evermore.

Hymns, Songs, and Spirituals

Use refrains of carols or single stanzas as the call to worship, offering response, during communion, or after the benediction.

Amen, amen (spiritual)

Gloria a Dios/Glory to God (trad. Peruvian)

Like a whisper in the heart (Dunstan, to GLORIA

Rise up, shepherd, and follow (spiritual)

Star-Child, Earth-Child (Murray)

The Virgin Mary had a baby boy (West Indian carol)

Litany of the Coming of the Christ Child

Response (R): The Child of God comes for them.

Precious in God's eyes are the shepherds on the hillside,   **R**

Precious in God's eyes are the refugees in the shelter,   **R**

Precious in God's eyes are the animals in the stable,   R

Precious in God's eyes are those who bring good things to birth,   R

Precious in God's eyes are those who steadfastly follow God's star,   R

Precious in God's eyes are the outcast and poor,   R

Precious in God's eyes are those

    who have no place to lay their heads tonight,   R

Precious in God's eyes are those who take courage to do the right,   R

Precious in God's eyes are those who are displaced by wars,   R

Precious in God's eyes are those in hospitals and hospices,   R

Precious in God's eyes are those who long to meet the Christ Child,   R

Precious in God's eyes are those who bring God's light to birth,   R

    Final response (R): The Child of God comes for us.

Memorial Acclamation for Communion

Christ was born, Christ has risen, Christ will come again with glory.

Candle lighting, see chapter 1

Preaching

Preaching for Christmas Eve and the days following: what gifts do we bring to the Christ Child who has brought us so many gifts—hope, salvation, unending love, incarnation, valuing of human life? An Orthodox prayer (see Simcoe, *Christmas Sourcebook*, 96) suggests that angels bring a song, the heavens bring a star, the town of Bethlehem gives a manger, the shepherds bring adoration, Mary gives herself, and the Magi bring gifts fit for a king. What might we offer in or to the world as a witness to God's incredible Gift to us?

Another way to counter the sometimes saccharine secular portrayal of Christmas as you prepare in Advent is to educate your congregation carefully on the scriptural accounts of the incarnation. What do Matthew and Luke really say? Why are Mark's and John's Gospels different in their opening chapters? To whom do angels appear? Who is silenced in the days before a birth? Where are the stories of the shepherds and of the Magi? Critical thinking and study can sustain us beyond a childhood faith and open us to deeper wonder.

Additional thoughts:

• God in human form, salvation for the world, light in our darkness— a showdown of political power (the emperor Tiberius and the census for purposes of taxation and conscription) and God's power: to whom will we choose to be loyal? (William O'Brien, "Peace on Earth? Getting at the True Politics of Christmas" in *The Progressive Christian* (November/ December 2008), 7-8.

• God who shows up with a family of refugees in a manger in a small town . . . can show up anywhere.

• Are we star-seekers like the Magi? Willing adventurers like the shepherds? Trusting like Joseph? Willing to share space in our lives like Mary?

• The One who is born on Christmas Eve has already created the stars and spun the planets, divided the day and night, and breathed life into all creation.

For additional inspiration, see the Christmas stories of Katherine Paterson written for her church for Christmas Eve (collected in *A Midnight Clear: Stories for the Christmas Season* [New York: Lodestar, 1995] and *Angels and Other Strangers: Family Christmas Stories* [New York: Crowell, 1979]), sermons by Martin Luther (Christmas day, 1520) and John Chrysostom (for Christmas morning, late fourth century), and poems by Langston Hughes, "Shepherd's Song at Christmas" (share as a choral reading, found among other places in *Carol of the Brown King: Nativity Poems* [New York: Atheneum, 1998]); Jean Janzen, "Instructions: 'For Epiphany'," in *Paper House* (Intercourse, Pa.: Good Books, 2008);

Dorothee Sölle, "In This Night," in *Revolutionary Patience* (Maryknoll, N.Y.: Orbis, 1984); and Howard Thurman, "The Work of Christmas: When the Song of the Angels Is Stilled," in *The Mood of Christmas* (New York: Harper & Row, 1973).

The Eleven Days of Christmas, December 26–January 5

Preaching, throughout These Days

Fulgentius, North African bishop (ca. 462–ca. 527), said, "Christ made love the stairway that would enable all Christians to climb to heaven. Hold fast to love, therefore, in all sincerity, giving one another practical proof of your love, and by your progress in Christ's way of love, make your ascent together. Go in love!" (Mary Ann Simcoe, ed. *A Christmas Sourcebook* [Chicago: Liturgy Training Publications, 1984], 73)

The First Sunday after Christmas

Scriptures, Hymns, Songs, and Spirituals (see also Hymns, Songs, and Spirituals above for "Christmas")

Note: Psalm 148 is used all three years—plan to read it responsively or sing "Praise Ye the Lord" (Cleveland) or "Praise to the Lord" (Klusmeier).

A Isa. 63:7-9; Ps. 148; Heb. 2:10-18; Matt. 2:13-23. These scriptures relate to the Feast of the Holy Innocents, officially celebrated on December 28. Lullay, la lu, thou little tiny child (trad. medieval carol); Joseph, son of an ancient king (Damon); I am standing, waiting (Murray)

B Isa. 61:10–62:3; Ps. 148; Gal. 4:4-7; Luke 2:22-40; Now let your servant go in peace (Duck); Like a child (Damon); Niño lindo/Child so lovely (trad. Venezuelan)

C 1 Sam. 2:18-20, 26; Ps. 148; Col. 3:12-17; Luke 2:41-52; Star-Child, Earth-Child (Murray); At the font we start our journey (Rowthorn). Painting: Jesus among the Teachers/Vie de Jesus Mafa (from northern Cameroon; *IW*, 1:27).

Elements of Worship (See Names and Adjectives above for Christmas Eve/Day)

Prayer, Year A, based on Jeremiah 31:15, quoted in Matthew 2:18

Help us, God who came as a child, to move toward the children

in our lives and in our world

who have less full and happy lives than we wish for the child Jesus.

Move us to raise voices of solidarity and hope,

to demand that basic needs be met,

that children be cared for and safe from harm.

Keep our ears open to the Rachels weeping in our own streets

and those around the world,

that we might bring the gifts of incarnation—

of love instead of hate, of peace instead of war,

of food instead of bombs.

One: God hears our prayer and our hopes for changed behavior.

God alone can give us the strength to change the weeping for children into action on their behalf. God alone can pour forgiveness out so that we can focus on others rather than ourselves.

Thanks be to God, we are forgiven already.

Many: Today we commit ourselves to hear the Word

and to be a voice of action and hope for the world's children.

Confession, Year B

Pull us back, O God, from holiday celebrations and downtime, back to you and your most incredible Gift of Love in Jesus Christ. We tend to be fickle, flitting from one thing to another, without grounding ourselves in your presence. Keep us focused on Christ Jesus that we may learn from you how to live.

Assurance of Pardon, Year B

Sisters and brothers, how much God must love us, to condense into the form of an infant of humble birth, among animals and poor shepherds! Yet the stars and angels, Simeon and Anna, could not contain their joy in proclaiming that God comes among us to bring peace. May that joy and peace grow this day in our hearts and radiate out from us.

Call to Worship (based on Colossians 3:12-17), Year C

One: God has come to us, clothed in human form,

skin and bones, to a time in our history.

Many: God knows what it is like to be human like us.

One: Let us now clothe ourselves with compassion and kindness,

with humility and patience, with love over all.

Many: Come, O God, and clothe us in the character of Christ.

The Second Sunday after Christmas

Scriptures, Hymns, Songs, and Spirituals

A, B, C: Jer. 31:7-14; Ps. 147:12-20; Eph. 1:3-14; John 1:(1-9), 10-18

There are still carols to sing, perhaps some of the ones that move us toward Epiphany: "The first Noel"; "Angels from the realms of glory"; "Break forth, O beauteous heavenly light"; "Good Christian friends, rejoice"; "Sing we now of Christmas."

Element of Worship

Collect

God who came to us in human flesh

and who comes now to us with the power of your Holy Spirit,

call us who are made in your image always to love

what is most deeply human,

as you do, so that human beings everywhere

might know how much they are loved and valued.

We pray in the power of your incarnation. Amen.

Epiphany, January 6, Celebrated on the Day or on the Sunday between January 2 and 8

Scriptures

A, B, C: Isa. 60:1-6; Ps. 72:1-7, 10-14; Eph. 3:1-12; Matt. 2:1-12

Preparation

This day is full of sparkling symbols: the constancy of the star that caught the eye of the Magi; the crowns of the Magi; gifts of gold, frankincense, and myrrh, probably given in treasure boxes or wrapped in fine cloth. The color of paraments and vestments for this day are white and gold. Visual options include Jan Brueghel the Elder's sixteenth-century painting "The Adoration of the Kings," showing all his known world coming to worship at the manger; and "The Adoration of the Magi" by Juan Bautista Maíno (1581–1649), which depicts various nationalities for the Magi.

Elements of Worship

Names and Adjectives for God Particularly Appropriate for Epiphany and the Following Season

Brightness of our dawn	Gift to the Gentiles
Christ, Beloved Son	Glory of our God
Christ, brightness of God's glory	God of perfect light
Christ, image of the everlasting God	God of sages and fools
Christ, true Light of God	God of the nations
Christ, Wisdom and Power of God	Guiding God
Creator of heaven and Presence on earth	Helper of the poor
Daystar	Morning Star

Eternal Light   Radiant God

Eternal Wisdom

Hymns, Songs, and Spirituals

Arise, shine, for your light has come (Smith)

As the dark awaits the dawn (Cherwien)

I sought him dressed in finest clothes (Bell)

Star-Child, Earth-Child (Murray)

The Virgin Mary had a baby boy (West Indian carol)

We invite all to join our circle wide (Aldredge-Clanton)

Calls to Worship

God's holy day has dawned for us at last.

Come, everyone, and praise God!

>   One: Creator of sunlight dancing on water,

>   **Many: your light beams now**

>   **in the midst of summer in the Southern Hemisphere.**

>   One: Creator of snow crystals,

>   **Many: your light sparkles now**

>   **in the midst of winter in the Northern Hemisphere.**

>   One: Creator who came among us, twinkling as a star,

>   shimmering like gifts of gold,

and bright as a newborn infant,

Many: shine on our world

>   **that we might walk in the light of your Christ!**

Collect

We are star-struck, radiant God, by your glory and graciousness to us:

Shine your light through us that we may point all peoples

to your ways through our living.

In the Holy Name of Jesus, we pray. Amen.

Doxology, by Thomas à Kempis (ca. 1380–1471 monk and writer), final stanza of "O, love, how deep, how broad, how high" to "DEO GRATIS, VENI CREATOR, VENI EMMANUEL" (changing the refrain to "... Emmanuel *has* come to thee...") or OLD 100th.

All glory to our Lord and God

for love so deep, so high, so broad;

the Trinity whom we adore

forever and forevermore.

Prayer Litany: *each petition is to be followed by silence, then the response*

Response: For you, O Jesus, are the Christ,

the wisdom and power of God.

We pray today for all who are longing for God.   ***R***

We pray today for all who seek welcome in their search.   ***R***

We pray today that God's light may shine afresh in our world.   ***R***

We pray today that all who seek will be led to God's light.   ***R***

We pray today for the weak, the confused, the ill, the dying,

that they may be comforted.   ***R***

We pray today for unity among all who follow Jesus Christ.   ***R***

We pray today that we may become lights for God

in the world this week.   ***R***

Preaching

In the light of Epiphany, consider the following pairs of questions:

• Who are the Gentiles of our day? Is our church acknowledging them as members of the body of Christ?

• Are we sparkling, light-filled Christians, ready to share the good news? What would it take for us to be so and do so?

• Are we living into the call of Christ in our life, echoing our baptismal vows? Are we bringing light and wholeness to where we live and work?

Augustine speaks of Christ as the cornerstone, "the peace of the two walls coming from very different directions, from circumcision (the Jewish shepherds) and uncircumcision (the magi)." Compare with Ephesians 3:1-12, especially verse 6. What does this say about our own day and various faiths coming together and working together?

For additional inspirations see the poems "The Journey of the Magi" by T. S. Eliot, "The Gift" by William Carlos Williams, "Instructions: 'For Epiphany'" by Jean Janzen (found in *Paper House*), and "The Queens Came Late" by Norma Farber.

Advent: Season of Hope and Expectation

Scriptures, Hymns, Songs, and Spirituals;
Occasional Worship and Preaching Comments

(See also general music for the season below under "Hymns, Songs, and Spirituals.")

Year A

• 1st Sunday: Isa. 2:1-5; Ps. 122; Rom. 13:11-14; Matt. 24:36-44; I want to be ready (spiritual); Soon and very soon (Crouch); Awake, O sleeper (Tucker)

• 2nd Sunday: Isa. 11:1-10; Ps. 72:1-7, 18-19; Rom. 15:4-13; Matt. 3:1-12; On Jordan's bank, the Baptist's cry (Coffin); Hail to the Lord's anointed (Montgomery); May the God of hope go with us every day/Canto de Esperanza (Schutmaat)

• 3rd Sunday: Isa. 35:1-10; Ps. 146:5-10 or Luke 1:46b-55; Jas. 5:7-10; Matt. 11:2-11; Go and tell John (Pfautsch); Toda la tierra/All earth is waiting (Taulè); My heart sings out with joyful praise (Duck)

• 4th Sunday: Isa. 7:10-16; Ps. 80:1-7, 17-19; Rom. 1:1-7; Matt. 1:18-25; You were a child of mine/Joseph's carol (Wren); Pues si vivimos/When we are living (anon.). Psalm: develop litany around repeated verses, 80:7: Restore us, O God of hosts; let your face shine, that we may be saved.

Year B

• 1st Sunday: Isa. 64:1-9; Ps. 80:1-7, 17-19; 1 Cor. 1:3-9; Mark 13:24-37; My Lord, what a morning/mourning (spiritual); People, look east (Farjeon); The Lord is my light (Taizé). Psalm: develop litany around repeated verse, 80:7 (see above).

• 2nd Sunday: Isa. 40:1-11; Ps. 85:1-2, 8-13; 2 Pet. 3:8-15a; Mark 1:1-8; Wild and lone the prophet's voice (Daw); Prepare the way of the Lord (Taizé); Toda la tierra/All earth is waiting (Taulè)

• 3rd Sunday: Isa. 61:1-4, 8-11; Ps. 126 or Luke 1:46b-55; 1 Thess. 5:16-24; John 1:6-8, 19-28; Hail to the Lord's anointed (Montgomery); When God restored our common life (Duck); Come, join in Mary's prophet-song (Tice)

• 4th Sunday: 2 Sam. 7:1-11, 16; Luke 1:46b-55 or Ps. 89:1-4, 19-26; Rom. 16:25-27; Luke 1:26-38; Sing of Mary, pure and lowly (Palmer); My heart sings out with joyful praise (Duck); Come, thou long-expected Jesus (Wesley)

Year C

• 1st Sunday: Jer. 33:14-16; Ps. 25:1-10; 1 Thess. 3:9-13; Luke 21:25-36; Prepare the way of the Lord (Taizé); Toda la tierra/All earth is waiting (Taulè). Signs and distress, confusion and roaring, fear and foreboding are promised in Luke, while Thessalonians has verses of prayer and blessing, thanks and hopes. These texts throw us into a chaotic world, a world not unlike our own. But they also express hopes for justice and righteousness, and the epistle reading holds us tight with its prayers that God would strengthen our hearts in holiness, for the promised coming is not for the faint of heart. Advent is a call to serve the ruler of the universe, whose love and justice are far beyond our scope.

• 2nd Sunday: Mal. 3:1-4; Luke 1:68-79; Phil. 1:3-11; Luke 3:1-6; Toda la tierra/All earth is waiting (Taulè); Now bless the God of Israel (Duck). Malachi asks who can endure the day of God's coming—do you have someone who might sing "But who may abide the day of God's coming," this passage from Handel's Messiah? As John wanders in the wilderness baptizing, he calls us to repentance and remembrance of our baptism—when did the congregation last remember and recommit to its baptismal life?

• 3rd Sunday: Zeph. 3:14-20; Isa. 12:2-6; Phil. 4:4-7; Luke 3:7-18; Wild and lone the prophet's voice (Daw); May the God of hope go with us every day/Canto de esperanza (Schutmaat). On the third Sunday of Advent, the prophets and epistle turn to joy and exultation as God's salvation is revealed in our midst (in both Zeph. 3 and the alternative Isa. 12 reading). It is John who picks up the difficult strain this week, calling us vipers and pointing out the necessity of sharing, fair business practices, and being content with our salaries.

• 4th Sunday: Mic. 5:2-5a; Luke 1:46b-55 or Ps. 80:1-7; Heb. 10:5-10; Luke 1:39-45, (46-55); My heart sings out with joyful praise (Duck); Come, join in Mary's prophet-song (Tice). The fourth Sunday of Advent brings the prophetic word through Mary's Magnificat, a song of great reversals. God turns our human tendencies upside down, so that the lowly and hungry might be lifted up.

Preparation

Color: Purple or blue? See chapter 1 under "color."

Hanging of the Greens: Many congregations celebrate the first Sunday of Advent with a meal and Hanging of the Greens festival, decorating the church with evergreens representing God's faithfulness, and making ornaments to take home.

Advent Wreath

See chapter 1 for history and preparation.

Litany of the Advent Wreath

Child: Why do we light the candles on this wreath?

Youth or Adult: To remind us that the Light of the world,
Jesus Christ, is drawing near to us.

Child: How many candles will we light this day?

Youth or Adult: __(#), because this is the ___(#) Sunday
of our waiting in Advent.

Child: What do we do while we are waiting?

Youth or adult: We hope and love, work for peace,
and dream of God's vision.

All: God of hope, help us walk in your light.

Scriptures about God and light; choose a different one each week: Gen. 1:1-5; Ps. 27:1, 13-14; 43:3-4; Isa. 9:2, 6-7; 42:6-7; 60:1-3; Matt. 5:14; Luke 15:8-10; John 1:1-5; 8:12; 12:35; 2 Cor. 4:6; Eph. 5:8; 1 Pet. 2:9; Rev. 21:22-26; 22:5

All: Come, O Jesus!

Sing refrain from "O Come, O Come, Emmanuel"

Chrismon tree: In 1957, Frances Kipps Spencer wanted to create ornaments appropriate for a "church" Christmas tree for Ascension Lutheran Church in Danville, Virginia (http://www.chrismon.org/site/chrismon.htm). She decided on monograms from the Greek letters for Christ, **Chrismons**—which include the Chi (X) Rho (P), IHC, Chi and Iota (I), Alpha (A) and Omega (Ω), and INRI, as well as symbols for Christ—crosses, crown, lily of the valley, fish, butterfly, and various symbols of the Trinity. (For additional symbols and their meaning, see one of the many books on Chrismon trees or Patricia Klein's *Worship without Words: The Signs and Symbols of Our Faith,* expanded ed. [Orleans, Mass.: Paraclete, 2006].) One way to not rush the season while still using a Chrismon tree is to slow the pacing down: the first week have only the tree with its bare branches, the second week add white lights, the third week add the Chrismons, and the fourth week add a large star on top (*Before the Amen: Creative Resources for Worship,* ed. Maren C. Tirabassi and Maria I. Tirabassi [Cleveland: Pilgrim, 2007], 4–6).

Artwork for Bulletins or Contemplation: "The Annunciation" (1898) by Henry Ossawa Tanner and the triptych of the Annunciation by Robert Campin (ca. 1380–1444).

Advent Hymns or Christmas Carols?

This is where the Advent/Christmas debate becomes most heightened in the church—will you sing Christmas carols through December as the secular world does or save them for Christmas and sing songs of waiting and prophecy and hope during Advent? While this book recommends the second, there are several ways to work with congregations, including singing at least two Advent hymns along with one Christmas carol in each service.

Other ideas include:

1. Easing in the singing of carols: for example, for the first and second Sundays sing only Advent carols, then on the third and fourth Sundays, begin with Advent hymns and use Christmas carols later in the service.

2. The United Methodist Church's Dean McIntyre at the General Board of Discipleship suggests singing Advent texts to Christmas tunes: for example, The King shall come to ANTIOCH (Joy to the world) Watchman; Tell us of the night to MENDELSSOHN (Hark! The herald angels sing); "Of the Father's love begotten" to W ZLOBIE LEZY (Infant holy). All can be accessed online at www.gbod.org.

Elements of Worship

Names and Adjectives for God Appropriate to This Season

Christ, firstborn of creation	Hope of the world
Christ, love song of God	Life-giving God
Christ, Promised One	Loving Source of all life
Christ, Word of blessing	Morning Star
Christ, Word of challenge	Mother of all Creation
Creator of the stars of night	Our End and Our Beginning
Glory yet Unseen	Present Mystery
God beyond our understanding	Pulse of love
God coming near	Radiant Dawn
God for whom we watch and wait	Redeemer of us all
God of hope	Revealed Love
God of our salvation	Silent Word
God of the loving Heart	Spirit of hope
God-promised One	Spirit who sustains our waiting
Heart's Desire	The Beginning of beginning
Hidden, Eternal, and Self-giving God	Womb of Being
	Wonder of wonders
Hidden Truth	Wonderful Counselor
Holy Center	Your people's everlasting Light

Prayer

Response: Amen! Come, Jesus!

Savior of the nations, come!   **R**

We wait and hope for you.   **R**

Shine in our chaos.   **R**

Break the chains of sin and death.   **R**

Renew the life of our world.   **R**

Bring us hope and justice.   **R**

Let us bear your Word to the world.   **R**

Hymns, Songs, and Spirituals

Songs of longing and waiting, from the Taizé Community, including "Wait for the Lord," "Within our darkest night," any of the Magnificat settings, "The Lord is my light," and "The Lord is my song."

"Prepare the way of the Lord" (round) from Taizé, moving from unison to four-part round over Advent's four weeks; "Prepare ye the way of the Lord," with "Long live God" from *Godspell* (Schwartz and Tebelak); versions of the Magnificat for congregational singing, including "My heart sings out with joyful praise" (Duck). Also "As the dark awaits the dawn" (Cherwien); "Come now, O Prince of peace" (Lee); "He [Christ] came down that we may have love" (Cameroon, trad.); "Like a child" (Damon); "Toda la tierra/All earth is waiting"/various translations (Taulé).

Doxology, sung to Veni Emmanuel, "O come, O come, Emmanuel," based on Coffin's "On Jordan's bank" (1736):

> All praise the Christ eternally
>> whose advent sets all people free;
> whom with our Creator we adore
>> and Spirit blest for evermore.
> Rejoice, rejoice, Emmanuel
>> shall come to thee, O Israel.

O Antiphons

Possibly as early as the seventh century, and increasingly through the medieval period, the church praised God on December 17 through December 23 using the **"Great O antiphons"** in evening prayer, preceding and following the Magnificat. Originally sung alternately by two choirs and drawn from Hebrew Scriptures, these names for God had particular meanings for Christians celebrating the birth of the Messiah.

The well-known Advent hymn "O come, O come, Emmanuel" was written to accompany the O antiphons, and many current hymnals include the spoken responses for between the stanzas. If you have daily worship during this time, use the antiphon for the day; if not, use the antiphons on the Sunday that falls during these days, or spread them throughout the season, perhaps as the call to worship to focus each week. If the hymn is known by your congregation, consider singing it with only handbells to give the pitch at the beginning of each line of the song. For additional inspiration, see Madeleine L'Engle's poem on the O antiphons, called "O Oriens," which is in the same meter as the plainsong hymn (*A Cry Like A Bell* [Wheaton, Ill.: Harold Shaw, 1987], 53–54).

Sections of a Eucharistic Prayer for Advent (Drawn from Year C, Luke 3:1-6)

Narrative of the wonderful works of God

> It is right, and a good and joyful thing,
>> always and everywhere to give thanks to you,
>> Almighty God, creator of heaven and earth.
>
> From the depths of the swirling darkness, you brought forth light.
> From the dust of the earth, you formed us in your likeness,
>> breathed life and love into our beings,
>> and called us "very good."
>
> When we turned our faces from you,
>> your love continued to embrace us,
>> calling us back to relationship with you.
>
> You sent your prophets to proclaim reconciliation

and to prepare the way for the One who would restore us.

And so, with your people on earth and all the company of
heaven

we praise your name and join their unending hymn.

Narrative of God's work in Christ

Holy are you, and blessed is your Son Jesus Christ,

who smoothes our rough places,

straightens our crooked places,

brings wholeness to our broken places,

and through whom all flesh may see your salvation.

(*continue with traditional institution narrative*) (Robin D. Dillon)

Preaching

All of these Advent scriptures cannot lead to a jolly Santa or simply a cooing baby in a sanitized stable. This is a powerful God whom we serve, who can come with intensity beyond our imagining. This is a God whose mercy is cleansing and healing, who stitches our brokenness back together if we will heed the call of prophets of old and new. Can you imagine an alternative Advent and Christmas this year—one that calls to deep justice, that is not tempted by siren songs of merchandise, that hears instead the cries of the truly needy among us? What will it take in your congregation to let the prophetic Word be heard?

How will we recognize you, Christ, today—as another driver who needs entrance into my lane? As the child fussing in the grocery line who needs, along with her parent, a kind smile? As a cause about which we might encourage lawmakers? In the burden that someone needs help carrying? In the one who needs us to not look away?

Two prisoners held by Nazis, Dietrich Bonhoeffer and Alfred Delp, wrote about Advent as the season of waiting and surrender to God in ways that can be helpful to us today, in *Letters and Papers from Prison* (New York: Macmillan, 1953, 1967) and *The Prison Meditations of Alfred Delp* (New York: Macmillan, 1966), respectively, referred to in Bill Kellermann, Seasons of *Faith and Conscience: Kairos, Confession, Liturgy (Seasons)* (Maryknoll, N.Y.: Orbis, 1991).

Inspiration Found in Poetry

"Christ Climbed Down," Lawrence Ferlinghetti, in *A Coney Island of the Mind* (New York: New Directions, 1958)

"That Nature is a Heraclitean Fire and of the comfort of the Resurrection," Gerard Manley Hopkins (1844–1889), with its line: "I am all at once what Christ is, since he was what I am."

"The Annunciation," Edwin Muir (1887–1959)

"First Coming," in *A Cry Like a Bell,* Madeleine L'Engle (1987)

"Handmaid of the Lord," in *A Midnight Clear,* Katherine Paterson (1995)

CHAPTER 4

GOD'S TIME IN THE GREEN SEASON

Joyce Ann Zimmerman suggests, in *The Ministry of Liturgical Environment* (Collegeville, Minn.: Liturgical Press, 2004, 70), using a light or muted green in the Northern Hemisphere after the Epiphany; a brighter summertime green immediately after Trinity Sunday; and a third, richer green in late August and early September.

Ordinary Time after the Epiphany

Missio Dei: Following the revelation of Jesus to the Magi (outsiders), Jesus' baptism gives the example of solidarity with others. The identification of Jesus as Messiah at the Transfiguration claims him as the one who shows us God's vision. The Sundays between these two celebrations are filled with stories of Jesus teaching, healing, and reaching out to the edges of society.

Blessing: May God, who promised the world a Messiah, and who kept this promise by sending Jesus Christ to live among us, strengthen and bless you to reach out to the world with this good news.

Sending: Go, equipped by the Holy Spirit, to tell the world by your actions and your very being that Jesus Christ is the one we have been longing for!

Baptism of Jesus Christ, Sunday after Epiphany

Preparation

The baptismal font of the church is an important visual center for this day. The color of the day is white, as a celebration of a Christological event.

Other visuals for this day include the older depictions of the baptism of Jesus by John in the Jordan, often with a dove representing the Holy Spirit, and light or a hand reaching down from the sky representing the First Person of the Trinity. More contemporary representations include "The River" by John August Swanson (b. 1938) and "The Baptism of Jesus Christ" by Pheoris West (b. 1950), which may be found in *Imagining the Word* [*IW*] (Cleveland: United Church Press, 1996, vols. 3 and 1).

Scriptures

Year A: Isa. 42:1-9; Ps. 29; Acts 10:34-43; Matt. 3:13-17; When Jesus came to Jordan (Pratt Green); From tents of night the sun comes forth (Bringle)

Year B: Gen. 1:1-5; Ps. 29; Acts 19:1-7; Mark 1:4-11; When Jesus came to Jordan (Pratt Green); The strong and gentle voice (Tice)

Year C: Isa. 43:1-7; Ps. 29; Acts 8:14-17; Luke 3:15-17, 21-22; When Jesus came to Jordan (Pratt Green); I have called you by your name (Damon)

Elements of Worship

Names and Adjectives Particularly Appropriate for God on This Day

Anointed One	Our Example
Friend of sinners	Spirit Dove
Messiah	Voice of God

Prayer

Holy Spirit, Bright Dove from Heaven,
   alight on our shoulders and give us your blessing.
Let us hear in the fluttering of your wings
   that voice which says "in you I am well pleased."
Holy Spirit, Bright Flame from above,

set us ablaze with your tongues of truth.

Let us see in the flickering of your eyes

a reflection of our worth in you.

Holy Spirit, Bright Water of Birth,

pour over our beings and wash us anew.

Let us feel in the swirling of your tides

a power to move mountains by your Word.

Amen. (Michele Lynne Holloway)

Hymns, Songs, and Spirituals for Renewal of Baptism

Take me to the water (spiritual); Remember and rejoice (Duck)

Call to Worship

Today Jesus steps into the waters of the Jordan and God stands in solidarity with sinners.

Doxology (may be sung to OLD 100TH, GIFT OF LOVE, or TALLIS' CANON)

Praise Christ, who went to be baptized,

praise Spirit, who as dove came down,

praise God, who said, "This is my Child,"

one Trinity, grace all around!

Preaching

This is a day to focus on the meaning of Jesus Christ being God's Messiah for us and for the world. In what ways do we need to renew our discipleship in order to be part of Jesus' bringing God's reign to earth?

Ordinary Time

If there are fewer Sundays of Ordinary Time that follow Epiphany due to Easter being earlier, the readings of the lectionary that are omitted are those at the end of the list, beginning by omitting the ninth Sunday after the Epiphany. See names and adjectives for God from the Epiphany section in chapter 3.

Year A—Themes of Call and Reconciliation

• 2nd Sunday after the Epiphany: Isa. 49:1-7; Ps. 40:1-11; 1 Cor. 1:1-9; John 1:29-42; Agnus Dei/Lamb of God (various settings)

• 3rd Sunday after the Epiphany: Isa. 9:1-4; Ps. 27:1, 4-9; 1 Cor. 1:10-18; Matt. 4:12-23; Two fishermen (Toolan); How perilous the messianic call! (Wren)

• 4th Sunday after the Epiphany: Mic. 6:1-8; Ps. 15; 1 Cor. 1:18-31; Matt. 5:1-12; Blest are they (Haas); You are the salt for the earth (Haugen)

• 5th Sunday after the Epiphany: Isa. 58:1-9a (9b-12); Ps. 112:1-9 (10); 1 Cor. 2:1-12 (13-16); Matt. 5:13-20; This little light of mine (spiritual); You are salt for the earth (Haugen)

• 6th Sunday after the Epiphany: Deut. 30:15-20; Ps. 119:1-8; 1 Cor. 3:1-9; Matt. 5:21-37; Christ has changed the world's direction (Murray); The love of God receives us (Damon)

• 7th Sunday after the Epiphany: Lev. 19:1-2, 9-18; Ps. 119:33-40; 1 Cor. 3:10-11, 16-23; Matt. 5:38-48; see hymns for previous week

• 8th Sunday after the Epiphany: Isa. 49:8-16a; Ps. 131; 1 Cor. 4:1-5; Matt. 6:24-34; Peace, be not anxious (Bringle); Praise our God above (Chao)

• 9th Sunday after the Epiphany: Deut. 11:18-21, 26-28; Ps. 31:1-5, 19-24; Rom. 1:16-17; 3:22b-28, (29-31); Matt. 7:21-29; 'Tis the old ship of Zion (spiritual); My hope is built on nothing less (Mote)

Year B—Themes of Call and Healing

• 2nd Sunday after the Epiphany: 1 Sam. 3:1-10, (11-20); Ps. 139:1-6, 13-18; 1 Cor. 6:12-20; John 1:43-51; Come and see (Hamm); Forward through the ages (Hosmer)

• 3rd Sunday after the Epiphany: Jonah 3:1-5, 10; Ps. 62:5-12; 1 Cor. 7:29-31; Mark 1:14-20; Two fishermen (Toolan); Would I have answered when you called? (Stuempfle)

• 4th Sunday after the Epiphany: Deut. 18:15-20; Ps. 111; 1 Cor. 8:1-13; Mark 1:21-28; Silence, frenzied, unclean spirit (Troeger); God has spoken by the prophets (Briggs)

• 5th Sunday after the Epiphany: Isa. 40:21-31; Ps. 147:1-11, 20c; 1 Cor. 9:16-23; Mark 1:29-39; O Christ, the healer (Pratt Green); When Jesus the healer passed through Galilee (Smith)

• 6th Sunday after the Epiphany: 2 Kgs. 5:1-14; Ps. 30; 1 Cor. 9:24-27; Mark 1:40-45; see hymns for previous week, using appropriate stanzas

• 7th Sunday after the Epiphany: Isa. 43:18-25; Ps. 41; 1 Cor. 1:18-22; Mark 2:1-12; see hymns for previous week, using appropriate stanzas

• 8th Sunday after the Epiphany: Hosea 2:14-20; Ps. 103:1-13, 22; 2 Cor. 3:1-6; Mark 2:13-22; Come and see (Hamm); I have decided to follow Jesus (anon.)

• 9th Sunday after the Epiphany: Deut. 5:12-15; Ps. 81:1-10; 2 Cor. 4:5-12; Mark 2:23–3:6; How perilous the messianic call! (Wren); Rise, shine, you people (Klug)

Year C—Themes of Call and Life Together

• 2nd Sunday after the Epiphany: Isa. 62:1-5; Ps. 36:5-10; 1 Cor. 12:1-11; John 2:1-11; Christ, whose glory fills the skies (Wesley); We all are one in mission (Edwards)

• 3rd Sunday after the Epiphany: Neh. 8:1-3, 5-6, 8-10; Ps. 19; 1 Cor. 12:12-31a; Luke 4:14-21; The Spirit sends us forth to serve (Dufner); Morning glory, starlit sky (Vanstone)

• 4th Sunday after the Epiphany: Jer. 1:4-10; Ps. 71:1-6; 1 Cor. 13:1-13; Luke 4:21-30; How perilous the messianic call! (Wren); Ubi caritas (Taizé)

• 5th Sunday after the Epiphany: Isa. 6:1-8, (9-13); Ps. 138; 1 Cor. 15:1-

11; Luke 5:1-11; Would I have answered when you called? (Stuempfle); Amen, Amen (spiritual) with verses

• 6th Sunday after the Epiphany: Jer. 17:5-10; Ps. 1; 1 Cor. 15:12-20; Luke 6:17-26; God, your knowing eye can see (Tice); Christ the Lord is risen (Colvin)

• 7th Sunday after the Epiphany: Gen. 45:3-11, 15; Ps. 37:1-11, 39-40; 1 Cor. 15:35-38, 42-50; Luke 6:27-38; Christ has changed the world's direction (Murray); The love of God receives us (Damon)

• 8th Sunday after the Epiphany: Isa. 55:10-13; Ps. 92:1-4, 12-15; 1 Cor. 15:51-58; Luke 6:39-49; My hope is built on nothing less (Mote); Christ the Lord is risen (Colvin)

• 9th Sunday after the Epiphany: 1 Kgs. 8:22-23, 41-43; Ps. 96:1-9; Gal. 1:1-12; Luke 7:1-10; O Christ, the healer (Pratt Green); When Jesus the healer passed through Galilee (Smith)

Sunday before Ash Wednesday, Transfiguration Sunday

Preparation

This is a day of dazzling light, so brighten the sanctuary, using white paraments and candles or other bright lights. Visual images include "Luminescence" by Ivan Kudriashev (sometimes spelled Kudryashov; 1926), or the wood carving "The Transfiguration" by Elijah Pierce (1892–1984), (*IW* 1 and 3).

Scriptures

A Exod. 24:12-18; Ps. 2 or Ps. 99; 2 Pet. 1:16-21; Matt. 17:1-9

B 2 Kgs. 2:1-12; Ps. 50:1-6; 2 Cor. 4:3-6; Mark 9:2-9

C Exod. 34:29-35; Ps. 99; 2 Cor. 3:12–4:2; Luke 9:28-36, (37-43)

Elements of Worship

Names and Adjectives for God Particularly Appropriate for This Day

Christ, Image of God	God of the mountaintops
Christ, the Beloved	God of the whirlwind

Christ, the Chosen One	God, who parts the waters
Dazzling Light	Messiah
God of Moses, God of Elijah,	Morning Star
God in Christ	Transfigured Christ

Hymns, Songs, and Spirituals

Shine, Jesus, shine (Kendrick); Swiftly pass the clouds of glory (Troeger); This little light of mine (spiritual) with verses: "Shine like Jesus shone, let's all let it shine..." and "Jesus is the Christ, let's all tell the world..."; We have come at Christ's own bidding (Daw)

Collect

Shining Christ, God's chosen and beloved,

brighten our gray days with your light and truth,

that we might understand who you really are

and be inspired and energized to follow you

from the mountaintops into our everyday lives.

We pray this in your name, Holy Trinity. Amen.

Preaching

In Transfiguration God is working to transfigure us like Jesus, so that we will be able to discern God's presence in the world and be empowered to follow God's will more courageously. Thomas Merton (1915–1968) said, "We are living in a world that is absolutely transparent, and God is shining through it all the time" (quoted in Marcus Borg, *The Heart of Christianity: Rediscovering a Life of Faith* [New York: HarperOne, 2004], 155). Barbara Brown Taylor's "Dazzling Darkness" reminds us that Moses not only represents the Law, but the moving toward freedom—with Jesus from fear of sin and death; Elijah not only represents the Prophets, but the one who is to come, the Messiah—who is Jesus, now glowing from fire within

(Barbara Brown Taylor, "Dazzling Darkness (Lk. 9:28-36)," *The Christian Century* (Feb. 4–11, 1998): 105). Note that 2 Corinthians 3:12-16, usually included in the lectionary for Year C, has anti-Semitic references, to which Christians are becoming increasingly sensitive.

Ordinary Time after Pentecost

If, in the Ordinary Time that follows Pentecost, there are fewer Sundays due to the lateness of Easter and thus Pentecost, the lectionary readings that are omitted are those at the beginning of the season, going directly to the date of the Sunday in question. All readings are for the Sunday that fall during the dates cited. During the summer, the *RCL* gives alternative Hebrew Bible readings; these have been included in chapter 5.

• Follow up the Spirit's red of Pentecost by having something red in the worship space each of the following Sundays. Have the children discover what and where it is each week, as you talk about looking for God's Spirit in scripture and in singing, in kindnesses and comforting moments, in sharing and being energized together. Where did you see the Spirit at work this week?

• Consider the resources given for Pentecost and the season following in chapter 2.

Missio Dei, for Trinity Sunday through June

The Trinity models for us a way of being together as church, as household, as neighborhood, and as world. We go into this season in the power of Pentecost to live in mutual love and respect for all creation.

Blessing (from 2 Cor. 13:13)
May the grace of Jesus Christ, the love of God,
and the fellowship of the Holy Spirit,
One God, now and forever, be with us all.

Sending
Go to live and love as God, the Holy Trinity, does:
in mutual love and respect, encouraging

and building up every person you meet.

Response: We are sent in the name of God!

Missio Dei, for July and August

Blessing

May God, who has created this incredible world

and who calls us as partners in creation, fill you with blessings.

May Jesus Christ, who saw the potential in each person,

grow in your life.

Sending

May the Holy Spirit, alive in baptismal waters,

in Pentecost wind and flame,

send you into the world to do God's will. Go, in the name of God!

Missio Dei, for September and October

Blessing

God has blessed you with abundance, with love, mercy, and grace.

Sending (based on Phil. 4:8)

So, beloved of God, whatever is true, and honorable, and just,

if there is any excellence and if there is anything worthy of praise,

think about these things and act on them for the glory of God's reign.

Missio Dei, for November

This month is framed by All Saints' Day and Reign of Christ Sunday, with Thanksgiving (in the United States) in between. All Saints' Day challenges everyone to live a holy life worthy of God's calling. Thanksgiving reminds us that, as 2 Corinthians 9:8 confidently states: "God is able to provide you with every blessing in abundance, so that by always having enough of everything, you may share abundantly in every good work."

Blessing

Children of God, inheritors of the promises made through Jesus Christ, know that you are blessed and beloved.

Sending (based on Ephesians 1:12)

Go out to live for the praise of God's glory.

May the Source of all good gifts go with you,

providing richly for your needs and, through you,

      for the needs of all the world.

Responses for Prayers or Litanies during Ordinary Time

God's love endures forever.

Listen, God is calling.

Loving God, **keep us faithful and believing.**

Your kingdom come; **your will be done on earth.**

For further inspiration see Jean Janzen's "Instructions: 'For Ordinary Time' " in *Paper House* (Intercourse, Pa.: Good Books, 2008).

Trinity Sunday

Preparation

The Greek description of the Trinity as **perichoresis** (see Leonardo Boff, Jurgen Moltmann, Elizabeth Johnson, and Catherine LaCugna) draws on its dancing fluidity of mutual relationality and calls to us to enter that experience, with God and with one another. The traditional color for this day is white. Visual art includes the traditional images of the Trinity: equilateral triangle, trefoil, **triquetra** (Celtic, three interlocking loops made of one continuous strand), three interlocking circles, or a circle (representing eternity and completeness) enclosing an equilateral triangle. (See Patricia Klein, *Worship without Words: The Signs and Symbols of Our Faith,* expanded ed. [Orleans, Mass.: Paraclete, 2006].)

Scripture and Hymns, Songs and Spirituals

See general suggestions below.

Year A

• Gen. 1:1–2:4a; Ps. 8; 2 Cor. 13:11-13; Matt. 28:16-20; Go in grace and make disciples (including verse 3 as doxology or sending forth) (Bringle); Give thanks for wolf and bird (Damon)

Year B

• Isa. 6:1-8; Ps. 29; Rom. 8:12-17; John 3:1-17; Santo, santo, santo (anon., Argentina); The play of the Godhead (Bringle)

Year C

• Prov. 8:1-4, 22-31; Ps. 8; Rom. 5:1-5; John 16:12-15; any of the songs listed above and Doxology from James Montgomery (1854), sung to DAVIS:

> Creator, Redeemer, and Spirit of Truth,
>
> One God over all evermore,
>
> Let all ages join with us here in this time,
>
> To honor, praise, love, and adore.

Elements of Worship

Names and Adjectives for God, Particularly Appropriate to This Day

Eternal and Incomprehensible God	Three in One
God in Three Persons	Three in One, One in Three
Holy undivided Trinity	Trinity of Love
Our One True God	

Hymns, Songs, and Spirituals

General

Breath of God, Breath of peace (Tice); God the Spirit, guide and guardian (Daw); Source and Sovereign, Rock and Cloud (Troeger); When we seek language to praise you, O God (Daw)

Doxology

Final stanza of Holy, Holy, Holy (Heber); You are holy (Harling)

Trinitarian Closing Doxology for Prayers

In the name of Jesus Christ, who lives and reigns with you and the Holy Spirit, one God, now and forever. Amen.

One tradition of the Christian church is to pray "**to** God [the First Person], **through** Jesus Christ, **by** the power of the Holy Spirit."

Collect

Triune God,

you are one in three and three in one,

our highest example of **community.**

Bring us to a place of nurturing togetherness

that we may experience the life-giving truth

of "I am because we are";

through Jesus who created community wherever he went. Amen.

(Michele Lynne Holloway)

Prayer of Adoration (to be said by one voice or many)

Before all time, you existed, Great God.

Before the earth had form and mass, before the sun shone,

the oceans roared, or stars twinkled, you were.

Birds have sung your praises, elephants trumpeted your name,

crickets chirped your glory, and dolphins swam to your delight.

At your command, Holy Trinity, trees put forth leaves,

flowers blossom, forests rise,

streams flow, and mountains take shape.

Your creativity set stars spinning, gave flight to eagles,

moved tides and planets, and guided animals to fresh food.

Three-in-One, you come to humanity in ways mysterious and ordinary—

through a sunset on fields, in the refreshing rain, in the bustle of cities,

in a gentle embrace, in truthful conversations, in the heat of debate,

in sleep-tossed nights or a sunny day, by our hospital beds,

in a moment of hope in a difficult situation,

    in spite of human betrayal,

in the color of a flower or the purr of a cat.

You loved us enough to come in flesh

    to share our human pain and struggle

and you rose to show the depths of that continuing love,

    in spite of our turning away.

When we retell the stories of your people in ancient times,

or experience you anew through communion bread and cup,

or feel the fire or whisper of your Spirit,

you communicate truth, righteousness, mercy, and love.

Thank you, Holy God,

Thank you, Mystery Beyond our Knowing,

Walker among Us, and Spirit of Love,

Three in One, Holy Trinity. Thank you!

Preaching

One of the challenges of discussing Trinitarian doctrine is our tendency to pull the Trinity apart into three distinct Persons without maintaining its essential undivided nature. Preaching on this day needs to not theologically or cerebrally dissect the doctrine of the Trinity, but instead to praise and give thanks for the many ways in which God calls us into the relationship of the Trinity (see "Prayer of Adoration" above; and Catherine LaCugna's "Making the Most of Trinity Sunday," in *BMH*, (Collegeville, Minn.: Liturgical Press, 2000), 247–261).

Scriptures; Hymns, Songs, and Spirituals; Occasional Comments for Theme, Preaching, or Art

Year A

• May 29–June 4, if after Trinity Sunday: Gen. 6:9-22; 7:24; 8:14-19; Ps. 46; Rom. 1:16-17; 3:22b-28, (29-31); Matt. 7:21-29; My hope is built on nothing less (Mote); Thanks be to God, our great salvation (Duck)

• June 5–11, if after Trinity Sunday: Gen. 12:1-9; Ps. 33:1-12; Rom. 4:13-25; Matt. 9:9-13, 18-26; Awake with timbrel and with dance (Bringle); Come, all who long for peace on earth (Duck)

• June 12–18, if after Trinity Sunday: Gen. 18:1-15, (21:1-7); Ps. 116:1-2, 12-19; Rom. 5:1-8; Matt. 9:35–10:8, (9-23); When Jesus the healer passed through Galilee (Smith); Together we serve (Damon)

• June 19–25, if after Trinity Sunday: Gen. 21:8-21; Ps. 86:1-10, 16-17; Rom. 6:1b-11; Matt. 10:24-39; How perilous the messianic call! (Wren); Be not afraid (Dufford)

• June 26–July 2: Gen. 22:1-14; Ps. 13; Rom. 6:12-23; Matt. 10:40-42; Cuando el pobre (Olivar and Manzano); In water we grow (Wren)

• July 3–9: Gen. 24:34-38, 42-49, 58-67; Ps. 45:10-17 or Song 2:8-13; Rom. 7:15-25a; Matt. 11:16-19, 25-30; Come, all of you (Laotian); Standing in the need of prayer (spiritual); All who hunger (Dunstan)

• July 10–16: Gen. 25:19-34; Ps. 119:105-112; Rom. 8:1-11; Matt. 13:1-9, 18-23; Thy word is a lamp unto my feet (Grant); "Abba, Abba, hear us," we cry (Donaldson); Sois la semilla/You are the seed (Gabaraín)

• July 17–23: Gen. 28:10-19a; Ps. 139:1-12, 23-24; Rom. 8:12-25; Matt. 13:24-30, 36-43; If I take the wings of the morning (Damon); O Holy Spirit, Root of life (Janzen); We are climbing Jacob's ladder (spiritual)

• July 24–30: Gen. 29:15-28; Ps. 105:1-11, 45b; Rom. 8:26-39; Matt. 13:31-33, 44-52; The kingdom of God (Grindal); Through our fragmentary prayers (Troeger)

• July 31–Aug. 6: Gen. 32:22-31; Ps. 17:1-7, 15; Rom. 9:1-5; Matt. 14:13-21; Let us be bread (Porter); Come, O thou Traveler unknown (Wesley)

• Aug. 7–13: Gen. 37:1-4, 12-28; Ps. 105:1-6, 16-22, 45b; Rom. 10:5-15; Matt. 14:22-33; Be not afraid (Dufford); When Cain killed Abel (Keithahn)

• Aug. 14–20: Gen. 45:1-15; Ps. 133; Rom. 11:1-2a, 29-32; Matt. 15: (10-20), 21-28; Oré poriaju (Guarani/Paraguay); How good (Duck)

• Aug. 21–27: Exod. 1:8–2:10; Ps. 124; Rom. 12:1-8; Matt. 16:13-20; Walk with me (Rice); A mother lined a basket (Keithahn); God, in your grace (Murray)

• Aug. 28–Sept. 3: Exod. 3:1-15; Ps. 105:1-6, 23-26, 45c; Rom. 12:9-21; Matt. 16:21-28; Beyond the bounds of space (Tice); We are standing on holy ground (Davis); Source and Sovereign, Rock and Cloud (Troeger). Some commentators suggest that the name given Moses might be translated, "I will be what tomorrow demands" (William C. Green, "Still-speaking Daily Devotionals," May 16, 2009, daily e-mails from the Writers Group of the United Church of Christ, http://www.ucc.org/feed-your-spirit/daily-devotional/). Art: "The Burning Bush" by Paul Koli (*IW*, 3:23, from *The Bible through Asian Eyes*, comp. by Masao Takenaka and Ron O'Grady [Auckland: Pace, 1991]).

• Sept. 4–10: Exod. 12:1-14; Ps. 149; Rom. 13:8-14; Matt. 18:15-20; The love of God receives us (Damon); Perdón, Dios/Forgive us, God (Lockward); "Forgive our sins as we forgive" (Herklots)

• Sept. 11–17: Exod. 14:19-31; Ps. 114 or Exod. 15:1b-11, 20-21; Rom. 14:1-12; Matt. 18:21-35; The love of God receives us (Damon); When Israel was in Egypt's land (spiritual); O Mary, don't you weep (spiritual). Exodus 15 art: "The Exodus with the Pillar of Fire" by Shalom of Safed (*IW*, 3:30–31 from *Images from the Bible: The Paintings of Shalom of Safed, the Words of Elie Wiesel* [Woodstock, N.Y.: Overlook, 1980]).

• Sept. 18–24: Exod. 16:2-15; Ps. 105:1-6, 37-45; Phil. 1:21-30; Matt. 20:1-16; Guide me, O thou great Jehovah (Williams); Who follows Jesus? (Tice)

• Sept. 25–Oct. 1: Exod. 17:1-7; Ps. 78:1-4, 12-16; Phil. 2:1-13; Matt. 21:23-32; All praise to thee (Tucker); Creator of the stars of night (anon.)

• Oct. 2–8: Exod. 20:1-4, 7-9, 12-20; Ps. 19; Phil. 3:4b-14; Matt. 21:33-46; Wake every breath and string! (Bringle); Joyful is the dark (verses 1, 2, 5) (Wren)

• Oct. 9–15: Exod. 32:1-14; Ps. 106:1-6, 19-23; Phil. 4:1-9; Matt. 22:1-14; Jubilate Deo (Taizé); Rejoice in God, all earthly lands (Duck)

• Oct. 16–22: Exod. 33:12-23; Ps. 99; 1 Thess. 1:1-10; Matt. 22:15-22; Rock of Ages, cleft for me (Toplady); Baited, the question rose (Daw)

• Oct. 23–29: Deut. 34:1-12; Ps. 90:1-6, 13-17; 1 Thess. 2:1-8; Matt. 22:34-46; Love the Lord your God (Strathdee); In faith we come together (Aldredge-Clanton); O God, our help in ages past (Watts)

• Oct. 30–Nov. 5, if All Saints' not observed on this day: Josh. 3:7-17; Ps. 107:1-7, 33-37; 1 Thess. 2:9-13; Matt. 23:1-12; Crashing waters at creation (Dunstan); Jesu, Jesu, fill us with your love (Colvin)

• Nov. 6–12: Josh. 24:1-3a, 14-25; Ps. 78:1-7; 1 Thess. 4:13-18; Matt. 25:1-13; A cloud of witnesses around us (Wren); Come and fill our homes with your presence (Chapman)

• Nov. 13–19: Judg. 4:1-7; Ps. 123; 1 Thess. 5:1-11; Matt. 25:14-30; Let us talents and tongues employ (Kaan); ¡Canta, Débora, Canta! (Cruz)

Year B

• May 29–June 4, if after Trinity Sunday: 1 Sam. 3:1-10, (11-20); Ps. 139:1-6, 13-18; 2 Cor. 4:5-12; Mark 2:23–3:6; God of endless life unfolding (Duck); Listen, God is calling (trad. Tanzanian)

• June 5–11, if after Trinity Sunday: 1 Sam. 8:4-11, (12-15), 16-20, (11:14-15); Ps. 138; 2 Cor. 4:13–5:1; Mark 3:20-35; Who is my mother? (Murray); Lord, may our prayer rise like incense in your sight (Haas)

• June 12–18, if after Trinity Sunday: 1 Sam. 15:34–16:13; Ps. 20; 2 Cor. 5:6-10, (11-13), 14-17; Mark 4:26-34; The kingdom of God (Grindal); When there is no star to guide you (Troeger); We walk by faith, and not by sight (Alford)

• June 19–25, if after Trinity Sunday: 1 Sam. 17(:1a, 4-11, 19-23), 32-49; Ps. 9:9-20; 2 Cor. 6:1-13; Mark 4:35-41; Ocean is a call to worship (Damon); You never saw old Galilee (Stuempfle)

• June 26–July 2: 2 Sam. 1:1, 17-27; Ps. 130; 2 Cor. 8:7-15; Mark 5:21-43; When Jesus the healer (verses 1, 3, 7) (Smith); Heal us, Emmanuel (especially verses 4 and 5) (Cowper)

• July 3–9: 2 Sam. 5:1-5, 9-10; Ps. 48; 2 Cor. 12:2-10; Mark 6:1-13; The Spirit sends us forth to serve (Dufner); Sent out in Jesus' name (anon.); Marching to Zion (Watts and Lowry)

• July 10–16: 2 Sam. 6:1-5, 12b-19; Ps. 24; Eph. 1:3-14; Mark 6:14-29; Like Miriam who danced to praise (Keithahn); The King of glory comes (Jabusch)

• July 17–23: 2 Sam. 7:1-14a; Ps. 89:20-37; Eph. 2:11-22; Mark 6:30-34, 53-56; Holy Presence, Holy Teacher (Murray); When Jesus the healer passed through Galilee (verses 1, 3, 7) (Smith); I will sing of the mercies of the Lord forever (Fillmore). "Look up and see salvation walking toward you" (Christina Villa, "Stillspeaking Daily Devotionals," September 1, 2009, daily e-mails from the Writers Group of the United Church of Christ, http://www.ucc.org/feed-your-spirit/daily-devotional/).

The following four weeks, when the texts from John's Gospel about Jesus as the Bread of Life are used, provide a wonderful time to have communion every week.

• Serve communion each week a different way, beginning with the most familiar for your congregation.

• Come to the altar rail to kneel as people are able and take the bread and juice.

- Come to receive by intinction as given the bread and cup.

- Receive communion in the pews as God comes to us where we are.

- Surround the church in a circle to receive or serve one another (especially easy in smaller worshiping congregations).

- Have the bread baked at church before worship.

- See *Just in Time! Communion Services* (Robin Knowles Wallace [Nashville: Abingdon, 2006]) for additional ideas, explanations, and prayers.

- July 24–30: 2 Sam. 11:1-15; Ps. 14; Eph. 3:14-21; John 6:1-21; We invite all to join our circle wide (Aldredge-Clanton); God of the world's great cities (Idle)

- July 31–Aug. 6: 2 Sam. 11:26–12:13a; Ps. 51:1-12; Eph. 4:1-16; John 6:24-35; Halle, halle, hallelujah (with verses) (Mulrain); Somos uno en Cristo (anon.); There is one Lord, one faith, one baptism (Taizé)

- Aug. 7–13: 2 Sam. 18:5-9, 15, 31-33; Ps. 130; Eph. 4:25–5:2; John 6:35, 41-51; Life-giving bread (Manalo); We meet as friends at table (Wren)

- Aug. 14–20: 1 Kgs. 2:10-12; 3:3-14; Ps. 111; Eph. 5:15-20; John 6:51-58; I am the Bread of Life (Toolan); Life-giving bread (Manalo); Come and see the ways of wisdom (Duck)

- Aug. 21–27: 1 Kgs. 8:(1, 6, 10-11), 22-30, 41-43; Ps. 84; Eph. 6:10-20; John 6:56-69; How good and lovely is the place (Duck); The incense of the morning air (Bringle)

- Aug. 28–Sept. 3: Song 2:8-13; Ps. 45:1-2, 6-9; Jas. 1:17-27; Mark 7:1-8, 14-15, 21-23; Lord, I want to be a Christian (spiritual); The lily of the valley (Fry)

- Sept. 4–10: Prov. 22:1-2, 8-9, 22-23; Ps. 125; Jas. 2:1-10, (11-13), 14-17; Mark 7:24-37; All my hope is firmly grounded (Neander); Saranam, saranam (trad. Pakistani); refrain of Only trust him/God (Stockton)

• Sept. 11–17: Prov. 1:20-33; Ps. 19; Jas. 3:1-12; Mark 8:27-38; From tents of night the sun comes forth (Bringle); Wake every breath and string! (Bringle). This week's readings mention teaching and learning, so it is a good time to dedicate your Christian education leaders. Beware, however, says James, as "not many of you should become teachers"; teaching is an awesome responsibility and can be a temptation to power and judgment. Hymns for education/formation include: Praise the Source of faith and learning (Troeger); Wisdom, far beyond our knowledge (Gibson); How firm a foundation (anon.).

Prayer (based on Ps. 19)

> The heavens tell of your glory, O God,
> > and all creation sings your praise.
>
> You created us in your image
> > and breathed into us your Spirit.
>
> You gave us tongues to speak of your light and your love,
> > and you give us words that we might encourage one another
> > and build up the body of Christ.
>
> We confess to you, O God,
> > that sometimes our words tear down instead of build up;
> > sometimes our words hurt instead of heal;
> > sometimes our words curse instead of bless.
>
> Forgive us, we pray.
>
> Open our eyes, our hearts, our minds, and our mouths
> > to your transforming power and love.
>
> We ask this in the name of your Son, Jesus the Christ. Amen.
>
> (Robin D. Dillon)

• Sept. 18–24: Prov. 31:10-31; Ps. 1; Jas. 3:13–4:3, 7-8a; Mark 9:30-37; Like a child (Damon); We walk by faith (Alford); We shall not be moved (spiritual). This week's gospel reading follows the theme of teaching with that of giving up power and authority, and opening oneself. God's call involves new ways of being, of seeing, of understanding.

• Sept. 25–Oct. 1: Esth. 7:1-6, 9-10; 9:20-22; Ps. 124; Jas. 5:13-20; Mark 9:38-50; The love of God receives us (Damon); Cuando el pobre (Olivar and Manzano). Use James 5:13, 15-16, as a call to confession and consider a time of prayer and anointing individuals with oil. Persons may be anointed with the sign of the cross on the forehead or back of the hand with olive oil or an appropriate balm. Anointing is not a sacrament, so it can be administered by anyone with the right intention. Hymns for healing include Heal me, hands of Jesus (Perry); Open your eyes to the image of God (Tice); You anoint my head with oil (Schwartz).

• Oct. 2–8: Job 1:1; 2:1-10; Ps. 26; Heb. 1:1-4; 2:5-12; Mark 10:2-16; Like a child (Damon); Child of blessing, child of promise (Cole-Turner); When Job the great was brought to tears (Tice)

• Oct. 9–15: Job 23:1-9, 16-17; Ps. 22:1-15; Heb. 4:12-16; Mark 10:17-31; You are salt for the earth (Haugen); Held in the shelter of God's wing (Bringle); When Job the great was brought to tears (Tice)

• Oct. 16–22: Job 38:1-7, (34-41); Ps. 104:1-9, 24, 35c; Heb. 5:1-10; Mark 10:35-45; Jesu, Jesu, fill us with your love (Colvin); Would you share my passion? (variation on Are you able [Marlatt]) (Bringle); A cloud of witnesses around us (Wren)

• Oct. 23–29: Job 42:1-6, 10-17; Ps. 34:1-8, (19-22); Heb. 7:23-28; Mark 10:46-52; When Jesus the healer (Smith); Bless the Lord, my soul (Taizé); From the whirlwind (Bringle)

• Oct. 30–Nov. 5: Ruth 1:1-18; Ps. 146; Heb. 9:11-14; Mark 12:28-34; Love the Lord your God (Strathdee); If all you want, Lord, is my heart (Troeger); From sacred love (Bringle)

• Nov. 6–12: Ruth 3:1-5; 4:13-17; Ps. 127; Heb. 9:24-28; Mark 12:38-44; If all you want, Lord, is my heart (Troeger); Take my life (Havergal); Blessed are those who fear the Lord (Idle)

• Nov. 13–19: 1 Sam. 1:4-20; 1 Sam. 2:1-10; Heb. 10:11-14, (15-18), 19-25; Mark 13:1-8; A mother lined a basket (verses 2 and 4) (Keithahn); Through silver veils of morning mist (Bringle)

Year C

• May 29–June 4, if after Trinity Sunday: 1 Kgs. 18:20-21, (22-29), 30-39; Ps. 96; Gal. 1:1-12; Luke 7:1-10; O Christ, the healer (Pratt Green); Tuya es la Gloria/We sing of your glory (trad.); These are the days of Elijah (Mark)

• June 5–11, if after Trinity Sunday: 1 Kgs. 17:8-16, (17-24); Ps. 146; Gal. 1:11-24; Luke 7:11-17; When Jesus the healer (Smith); I'll praise my Maker while I've breath (Watts); These are the days of Elijah (Mark)

• June 12–18, if after Trinity Sunday: 1 Kgs. 21:1-10, (11-14), 15-21a; Ps. 5:1-8; Gal. 2:15-21; Luke 7:36–8:3; A woman poured her jar of rich perfume (Tice); Woman in the night (verses 5 and 6/house and road) (Wren); These are the days of Elijah (Mark)

• June 19–25, if after Trinity Sunday: 1 Kgs. 19:1-4, (5-7), 8-15a; Ps. 42; Gal. 3:23-29; Luke 8:26-39; When Jesus the healer (verses 1, 5, 7) (Smith); The thirsty deer longs for the streams (Mulrain); Come and find the quiet center (Murray)

• June 26–July 2: 2 Kgs. 2:1-2, 6-14; Ps. 77:1-2, 11-20; Gal. 5:1, 13-25; Luke 9:51-62; Stand, O stand firm (trad. Cameroonian); Swing low, sweet chariot (spiritual)

• July 3–9: 2 Kgs. 5:1-14; Ps. 30; Gal. 6:(1-6), 7-16; Luke 10:1-11, 16-20; Not alone, but two by two (Daw); Send me, Lord (trad. South African); There'll be joy in the morning (Sleeth)

• July 10–16: Amos 7:7-17; Ps. 82; Col. 1:1-14; Luke 10:25-37; A man had been robbed of all he had (Pratt Green); Let justice roll down like a river (Gibson)

• July 17–23: Amos 8:1-12; Ps. 52; Col. 1:15-28; Luke 10:38-42; Awake with timbrel and with dance (Bringle); Let justice roll down like a river (Gibson)

• July 24–30: Hos. 1:2-10; Ps. 85; Col. 2:6-15, (16-19); Luke 11:1-13; settings of The Lord's Prayer; Canticle of prayer (Luff and Routley); We know that Christ is raised (Geyer)

• July 31–Aug. 6: Hos. 11:1-11; Ps. 107:1-9, 43; Col. 3:1-11; Luke 12:13-21; Thank you, Lord (trad.); One bread, one body (Foley); In Christ there is no east or west (Oxenham)

• Aug. 7–13: Isa. 1:1, 10-20; Ps. 50:1-8, 22-23; Heb. 11:1-3, 8-16; Luke 12:32-40; Have no fear, little flock (Zimmermann and Jilson); Awake, O sleeper (Tucker)

• Aug. 14–20: Isa. 5:1-7; Ps. 80:1-2, 8-19; Heb. 11:29–12:2; Luke 12:49-56; Faith, while trees are still in blossom (Frostenson); When God restored our common life (Duck); What does the Lord require of you? (Strathdee)

• Aug. 21–27: Jer. 1:4-10; Ps. 71:1-6; Heb. 12:18-29; Luke 13:10-17; Tell us, Rabbi, is it lawful (Bringle); Blessed is the body and soul (Damon); Saranam, saranam (trad. Pakistani)

• Aug. 28–Sept. 3: Jer. 2:4-13; Ps. 81:1, 10-16; Heb. 13:1-8, 15-16; Luke 14:1, 7-14; As we gather at your table (Daw); O God beyond all praising (Perry)

• Sept. 4–10: Jer. 18:1-11; Ps. 139:1-6, 13-18; Phlm. 1-21; Luke 14:25-33; God of endless life unfolding (Duck); You, Creator God, have searched me (Mulrain)

• Sept. 11–17: Jer. 4:11-12, 22-28; Ps. 14; 1 Tim. 1:12-17; Luke 15:1-10; God's great love is so amazing (Gillette); Kyrie eleison (Taizé). See "Prayer," Luke 15:11b-32, Year C, Fourth Sunday in Lent in chapter 2.

• Sept. 18–24: Jer. 8:18–9:1; Ps. 79:1-9; 1 Tim. 2:1-7; Luke 16:1-13; There is a balm in Gilead (spiritual); When we are tested and wrestle alone (Duck)

• Sept. 25–Oct. 1: Jer. 32:1-3a, 6-15; Ps. 91:1-6, 14-16; 1 Tim. 6:6-19;

Luke 16:19-31; On eagles' wings (Joncas); What does the Lord require of you? (Strathdee); Rich man Dives/Poor man Lazarus (spiritual)

• Oct. 2–8: Lam. 1:1-6; Ps. 137; 2 Tim. 1:1-14; Luke 17:5-10; In what strange land (Murray); By the waters of Babylon (anon.); The kingdom of God (Grindal)

• Oct. 9–15: Jer. 29:1, 4-7; Ps. 66:1-12; 2 Tim. 2:8-15; Luke 17:11-19; An outcast among outcasts (Leach); Oré poriaju (Guarani/Paraguay); We sing of your glory/Tuya es la gloria (trad.)

• Oct. 16–22: Jer. 31:27-34; Ps. 119:97-104; 2 Tim. 3:14–4:5; Luke 18:1-8; Thy word is a lamp unto my feet (Grant); I will set my bow in the clouds (Damon)

• Oct. 23–29: Joel 2:23-32; Ps. 65; 2 Tim. 4:6-8, 16-18; Luke 18:9-14; Kyrie eleison (various); Where is the Miriam, where is the Moses? (Murray)

• Oct. 30–Nov. 5: Hab. 1:1-4; 2:1-4; Ps. 119:137-144; 2 Thess. 1:1-4, 11-12; Luke 19:1-10; Zacchaeus in the pay of Rome (Pratt Green); Thy word is a lamp unto my feet (Grant)

• Nov. 6–12: Hag. 1:15b–2:9; Ps. 145:1-5, 17-21; 2 Thess. 2:1-5, 13-17; Luke 20:27-38; Tell us, Rabbi, is it lawful (Bringle); Praise to God who gives us courage (Beall)

• Nov. 13–19: Isa. 65:17-25; Isa. 12; 2 Thess. 3:6-13; Luke 21:5-19; Praise to God who gives us courage (Beall); Surely it is God who saves me (White); O day of peace that dimly shines (Daw)

World Communion Sunday, First Sunday in October

Preparation

Using a variety of breads from around the world and handing the bread and cup to one another with care remind us of the community God calls us to be.

All Saints

Preparation

Since this is a day to particularly lift up those in the congregation who have died in the previous year, be in touch with their families and loved ones to prepare them. Since this day is farther from the death than the funeral, Laurence Hull Stookey suggests that "survivors will have begun to work through their grief and can hear the resurrection hope with greater clarity" (*Calendar: Christ's Time for the Church* [Nashville: Abingdon, 1996], 148). All Saints' Day has multiple scripture passages to choose from: the raising of Lazarus; the new heaven and earth of Revelation, Isaiah, and Daniel who remind us that we are held in God's hand; and two sets of Beatitudes. Many churches toll bells or light candles as the names of the dead are read, and then celebrate with the communion of saints at the communion table. For Year A, palms, from the Revelation 7 reading, are an appropriate symbol.

Visuals for All Saints include the energetic "Allerheiligen/All Saints Day" by Wassily Kandinsky (original source: Städtische Galerie im Lenbachhaus, Munich, Germany) or "Visit to the Departed" by Haitian artist Gerárd Valcin or the graphic "Judgment Day" by Aaron Douglas, originally an illustration for James Weldon Johnson's poem "The Judgment Day" in *God's Trombones* (*IW*, 3:20, 63, and 76). In addition to Johnson's poem, consider "The Saints Are Standing Row on Row," Gracia Grindal's translation from the Dutch, with a wide variety of saints named (originally published in *Liturgy: All Saints among the Churches: The Journal of the Liturgical Conference* 12:2 [Fall 1994], found in *IW*, 3:65).

Elements of Worship

Names and Adjectives for God, Particularly Appropriate for This Day

Christ, who raised Lazarus from the dead

God who calls us all to be saints
God who shines in glory

God of all the faithful	Our Alpha and Omega
God of heaven and earth	Sanctifying God
God of Mary and Martha	Sustaining God

Call to Worship

Welcome to this place where God calls us all to be saints,

to be persons who follow the holy way shown by Jesus Christ.

Collect

Sanctifier of the faithful,

> who called and sustained holy people

> in every age and place,

make us holy, generous, and loving,

> that we may dwell in you now and forever,

as part of your great cloud of witnesses,

> known as friends of Jesus Christ.

Through the power of your Holy Spirit,

> we pray to you, Holy Trinity. Amen.

Litany of Thanksgiving (*might be done as beginning of communion service*)

Response: For all your saints, we give you thanks.

For Abraham, Sarah, Noah, Moses, Miriam, Deborah, Samuel, David, the psalmists, and the prophets.   **R**

For Mary, Joseph, Anna, Simeon, the disciples, Peter, Paul, Lydia, Phoebe, Timothy, and the gospel writers.   **R**

For the early martyrs, for Augustine, Theresa, Francis and Claire, Julian, Thomas Aquinas, those who translated the Bible into the people's languages, Luther, Calvin, and _____ [*your church's founders*].   **R**

For the long train of unnamed friends of Jesus, from the earliest centuries of the church up through those we know.   **R**

For those who have died from this congregation in this past year [*name them*].   **R**

For those who died who have inspired us to live more faithful, we remember aloud. [*leave time for names, then respond*]   **R**

For those who remain in our hearts silently. [*Leave time for silence, then respond.*]   **R**

For all your saints, **we give you thanks. God, help us be numbered among your saints.**

Another option is to call saints to stand with us, beginning in history and moving to present day, with response "Stand with us now" or the Spanish "¡Presente!"

Communion: celebrates the church on earth and in heaven at one table.

Hymns, Songs, and Spirituals

General

Come, let us join our friends above (Wesley); Forward through the ages (Hosmer); I sing a song of the saints of God (Scott); I'm gonna live so God can use me (spiritual); Rejoice in God's saints (Pratt Green)

Year A: Come, now the feast is prepared (Bringle); Taste and see (Moore)

Year B: Eat this bread and never hunger (verse on Lazarus) (Damon); When Jesus learned his friend had died (Tice); Behold, behold, I make all things new (Bell)

Year C: Be not afraid (Dufford)

Preaching

Brother Alois of Taizé suggests that this day is not simply about remembering the past, nor looking inward, but that it calls us to reach out to those on the margins. "Choosing holiness does not necessarily mean to do more. The step forward to which we are called is to love more. And since love needs all our being to express itself, it is up to us to find ways, without waiting a single moment, of being more attentive to our neighbor" as described by Jesus in the story of the Good Samaritan ("All Saints Day: 'I Call you Friends,' " http://www.taize.fr/en_article9190.html).

Thanksgiving

Preparation

Some interdenominational and interfaith services grow out of clergy groups that are already meeting for support, spiritual growth, and communal cooperation; others grow out of partnerships between two or more congregations. Either way, those planning services will need to discuss actions and texts ahead of time to make sure that everyone can feel included. Christians in interfaith settings should consider carefully any language about the Trinity and Jesus Christ. Working across denominational lines and focusing on common language and music will ease your work together. If this is a strictly Christian service, consider having communion together if at all possible, as **Eucharist,** one name for communion, comes from the Greek word for giving thanks. Red or green are suitable colors for the day, as well as seasonal/harvest colors from your part of the globe. Since the service is focused on thanks to God, signs of agricultural bounty and nature along with other blessings are appropriate, whether your church is urban, rural, or in-between. The primary work of the host congregation in a multicongregational service will be offering generous and welcoming hospitality.

Scriptures; Hymns, Songs, and Spirituals

Sermon comments; see also general music below.

A Deut. 8:7-18; Ps. 65; 2 Cor. 9:6-15; Luke 17:11-19; An outcast among outcasts (Leach); Praise our God above (Chao); 2 Cor. 9:8: "And God is able to provide you with every blessing in abundance." Why? "So that by always having enough of everything, you may share abundantly in every good work."

B Joel 2:21-27; Ps. 126; 1 Tim. 2:1-7; Matt. 6:25-33; Peace, be not anxious (Bringle); Seek ye first (Lafferty); Matt. 6:33: Keep our focus on God's vision and God's righteousness.

C Deut. 26:1-11; Ps. 100; Phil. 4:4-9; John 6:25-35; Halle, halle, hallelujah (with verses) (Mulrain); I am the Bread of Life (Toolan); Rejoice in God, all earthly lands (Duck)

A Prayer for a Home Thanksgiving Dinner

One simple tradition is to have each person (all ages) name something for which she or he is thankful, and all respond after each naming with "Thank you, God."

Elements of Worship

Names and Adjectives, Particularly Appropriate for God on This Day

Bread of Heaven	God who blesses with abundance
Generous God	Satisfier of the needs of the world
Giving God	Source of all good gifts

Hymns, Songs, and Spirituals

These might be sung during a time of prayer (in the style of Taizé) of deep thanksgiving for individual needs met, for health, friends, life, work, school, family, home, church, Christ, the Spirit, Godself: Oré poriajú/Kyrie eleison (Guarani/Paraguay); Santo, santo, santo/Holy, holy, holy (Argentina); Thank you, Lord (trad.).

Offering: Consider giving the offering to a local food or shelter program, particularly one that reaches across denomination and faith lines. During the offertory prayer, lift up those ministries for God's blessing.

Preaching

Thanksgiving suggests a time for testimonies of thanks to God, instead of a one-person sermon, as gratitude is an important spiritual practice for everyone. Mention this plan before the service so the congregation might be thinking about and coming forth with thoughts ready.

Reign of Christ/Christ the King Sunday

Preparation

As this is a Christological festival, its color is white, with gold accents, although tones of green may still be present or hints of purple, symbolizing royalty. Visual symbols include a crown, orb, or scepter, alone or combined with the cross. See also the many icons, images, and paintings of Christ as the ruler of all, called Christ the Pantocrator.

Scriptures; Hymns, Songs, and Spirituals

See also general music below.

A Ezek. 34:11-16, 20-24; Ps. 100; Eph. 1:15-23; Matt. 25:31-46; Here am I (Wren); Bring forth the kingdom (Haugen); Jubilate Deo (Taizé)

B 2 Sam. 23:1-7; Ps. 132:1-12, (13-18); Rev. 1:4b-8; John 18:33-37; Halle, halle, hallelujah (trad. Caribbean); O God, beyond all praising (Perry); We sing to you, O God (Grindal)

C Jer. 23:1-6; Luke 1:68-79; Col. 1:11-20; Luke 23:33-43; Jesus, remember me (Taizé); Now bless the God of Israel (Duck); We are God's people (Leech)

Elements of Worship

Names and Adjectives for God, Particularly Appropriate for This Day

Alpha and Omega	God of power and love
Ancient, Present, and	Judge of all nations
Future One	Most high God

Christ of glory   Ruler of every heart and mind

Christ of truth   Sovereign Christ

Gate of heaven

Hymns, Songs, and Spirituals

General

Eternal Christ, you rule (Damon); O Christ, your loving power confounds (Bringle); The kingdom of God is justice and peace (Taizé); You, Lord, are both Lamb and Shepherd (Dunstan)

Preaching

Does our loyalty lie with Christ, or have we gotten mixed up with things of the world, ideas, institutions, fads, or habits that draw us away from living for the reign of Christ?

CHAPTER 5

ADDITIONAL IDEAS

There are many additional practices linked with the Christian year, for example, the Jesse tree for Advent, the symbolism of various flowers and greenery throughout the year, the Moravian Advent star, and Mardi Gras or Shrove Tuesday. Because of the nature of these elements and the length of this book, it is not possible to treat them all here. For symbolism throughout the Christian year, see Patricia Klein's *Worship without Words* (expanded ed. [Orleans, Mass.: Paraclete, 2006]).

In the early centuries of the church, evening-long services of waiting and prayer, known as vigils, were held in connection with the major holy days when baptisms took place, Easter, Epiphany, and Pentecost. Vigils generally included a ritual of candle lighting, reading of the Word, baptism, and communion. This pattern may still be seen in the Easter Vigil (chapter 2) and in parts of Christmas Eve services popular in North America today (see "Candle lighting" in chapter 1). The canticle most closely associated with all the vigils is the Te Deum Laudamus, probably by the fourth-century bishop Niceta of Remesiana, in present-day Serbia. This canticle begins, in English: "We praise You, O God. We acclaim you as Sovereign; all creation worships you." If your congregation has found the Easter Vigil meaningful, you might consider doing something similar before celebrating baptisms. See also information on the Epiphany Vigil, below.

THE PASCHAL CYCLE

Easter symbols: Other symbols used historically at Easter include the passionflower, peacock (symbol of Christ's resurrection, seen in annual shedding and regrowth of bird's plumage), pelican, phoenix (bird that rises from the ashes), and pomegranate (seeds bursting out represent Christ bursting from the tomb), and eggs for new life (and missed during the Lenten fast). See Klein's *Worship without Words* for further explanations.

The days before Ascension in the medieval church were marked by **Rogationtide** processions indicating the boundaries of the parish and invoking God's blessing on seedtime. Local custom gave focus to each local ritual during this time. The popularity of Rogationtide was not immediately suppressed by the Reformation, and it flourished for quite a while in Germany and England (Frank C. Senn, *The People's Work* [Minneapolis: Fortress, 2006], 165). Rural congregations may want to consider a weekend time of praise and prayer for planting.

The twelfth day after Passover, the twenty-seventh of Nisan in the Jewish calendar, has been marked since 1951 as **Holocaust Memorial Day.** Coming in the midst of the Great Fifty Days, it challenges us to consider the various questions the Holocaust raises about evil and about our own anti-Semitism.

Earth Day, celebrated on April 22 each year since 1970, is often mentioned in worship, giving thanks for creation and repenting of our misuse. It need not take away from celebration of the Great Fifty Days.

Lent

Occasionally, older liturgical books use the names for the Sundays before Lent begins: **Septuagesima** (seventy days before Easter), **Sexagesima** (sixty days before Easter), and **Quinquagesima** (fifty days before Easter) (note that the counting isn't exact). These Sundays gave the church from the sixth century on a way of easing into the disciplines of Lent.

Holy Week

Latin for linking with the traditions of the church on Palm/Passion Sunday: *Benedictus qui venit in nomine Deus!*/Blessed is the one who comes in the name of God!

Following Palm/Passion Sunday, scriptures are set in the *RCL* for worship each day of Holy Week, though current observance focuses on Holy/Maundy Thursday and Good Friday. There is strong tradition from early times of reading Judas's plot to betray Jesus on Wednesday of this week.

Throughout history, and still in the Roman Catholic Church, *liturgical oils* are blessed on Holy Thursday. James F. White mentions the traditions of olive oil for baptism and for healing and of olive oil and balm for confirmation (*Introduction to Christian Worship*, 3rd ed. [Nashville: Abingdon, 2000], 59).

Stations of the Cross or **Way of the Cross** has long been a devotional practice of Christians (individual or corporate) on Good Friday or during Lent, with scripture, prayers, procession, and music. A series of fourteen stations—nine biblical and five legendary—was stabilized by Pope Clement XII in 1731. Some churches have banners or paintings of the stations; many Roman Catholic churches have the stations incorporated into the design of the sanctuary. This event has been elaborated in Hispanic practice and in the United States, beginning in the 1970s, by social justice organizations, both conceiving it as a street processional with teaching, proclamation, and prayer, using as stations prison, business headquarters, and city hall, along with soup kitchens, food pantries, free health clinics, and shelters for the homeless. Instead of using stations, some congregations combine the prayer of this day with deeds for the world that reflect the servanthood of Jesus. Services for the Way of the Cross are available in worship books and by Daniel Berrigan; Leonardo Boff; Romano Guardini; the Iona Community (*Stages on the Way* [Chicago: GIA, 2000], 152–157); Mother Teresa of Calcutta and Brother Roger of Taizé; Thomas H. Troeger and William Rowan (*Not My Will but Yours Be Done* [Chicago: GIA, 1995]; see also David Tripp, "The Stations of the Cross: An Additional Version," in *Sacramental Life* (Ordinary Time 2000): 108–109). The spiritual "Were you there?" can easily be worded for each of the traditional fourteen stations or for the nine that are biblical. *El Vía Crucis de Jesús Migrante/The Way of the Cross of the Migrant Jesus* by Gioacchino Campese, C.S. (Liguori, Mo.: Libros Liguori, 2006) takes the story of Jesus from the flight to Egypt when he was an infant through thirteen stations around the events of Holy Thursday and Friday, ending with the risen Christ accompanying his disciples on the road.

Potential Congregational Responses for Stations of the Cross

We adore your cross, O Christ, and praise your resurrection.

For through the cross, joy has come to the whole world.

Christ walked this path for us. Thanks be to God.

Sing the refrain of "Let us break bread together": "O Lord, have mercy on me."

The Incarnational Cycle

Blue Christmas or Longest Day service: Some churches have sensed a pastoral need for a service during Advent or the Twelve Days of Christmas for those who are particularly sad during this time, for those who have lost loved ones recently, and for those who are lonely. The service consists of scriptures recalling God's promises of hope, prayers that the presence of God might be recognized in the midst of grief, and songs of healing. Songs might include: Come and fill our hearts (Taizé); Kum ba yah (spiritual, with appropriate verses); Into my heart (Clarke); Stay with us (Brokering); O Lord, hear my prayer (Taizé); O come, O come, Emmanuel.

Las Posadas, December 16–24: This celebration comes from Latin America, particularly from Puerto Rico and Mexico, as individuals representing Mary and Joseph seek shelter each of the nine nights before Christmas. Several denominations have included one-time versions of the liturgy of Las Posadas for inclusion in worship services during Advent or Christmas (see The United Methodist *Book of Worship* [Nashville: The United Methodist Publishing House, 1992], #267 for Advent; #281 for Christmas Eve; or the United Church of Christ website [www.ucc.org]). These liturgies are particularly tied into *missio Dei,* as they call us to consider the situations of refugees, the homeless, the hungry, and the poor. Visual art connected to Las Posadas includes *luminaria* (candles in sand in metal holders, paper bags, or clear plastic jugs that light a walkway).

Mary's and Hannah's prayer songs: The prayer of Hannah in 1 Samuel 2:1-10 provided a model for Mary's prayer in Luke 1:46b-55, known as the **Magnificat/**My soul magnifies God. While Mary's song appears in each of the lectionary years for Advent (3rd Sunday of Advent Year A, 3rd or 4th Sunday Year B, and 4th Sunday Year C), Hannah's song only appears in the *RCL* as an option for the Psalm reading on the Sunday during November 13 through 19 in Year B. Those churches that are seeking to strengthen their historic connection with Hebrew Scripture and faith might include Hannah's song as counterpoint and harmony for Mary's song during Advent each year.

Services of Lessons and Carols, Advent or Christmas: This tradition began in England in the 1800s and gathered wider use after it was used in King's College Chapel, Cambridge, Great Britain, in 1918. Scripture readings, telling of God's reaching out to reconcile with humanity, combine with carols and prayer. This service has the advantage over choral cantatas of more congregational participation and often a stronger scriptural base; choirs can add a stanza of four-part singing, teach a new carol, and add descants; other musical instruments can be included as well. This format can work well either for congregations seeking to learn new Advent carols or those who can't wait for Christmas to sing Christmas carols. See The United Methodist *Book of Worship* (Nashville: The United Methodist Publishing House, 1992), #263 for an Advent version, #284 for a Christmas version; *Chalice Worship* (St. Louis: Chalice, 1997), 98, is suggested for either Advent or Christmas. Additionally, if you decide to use Latin for linking with the traditions of the church on Christmas Eve or Day, the following phrase is appropriate for either day: *Hodie, Christus natus est!* Today Christ is born!

The mystery of incarnation: Fred Pratt Green wrote the hymn, Mary looks upon her child/Birth Is a Mystery contemplating the picture of the Nativity, "The Newborn Child," by Georges de la Tour (1593–1652).

Stephen, deacon and martyr, December 26: Stephen (Acts 6:5, 8-15) was the first Christian martyr (Acts 7:54–8:2). His symbols include stones and a cloak; the color for the day is red. The reading of the stoning of Stephen also appears in the *RCL* for the 5th Sunday of Easter in Year A. Scriptures are Jer. 26:1-9, 12-15; Ps. 31:1-5; Acts 6:8–7:2a, 51c-60; Matt. 23:34-39. Hymns include: When Stephen, full of power and grace (Struther); By all your saints still striving (Nelson, stanza about Stephen).

John, apostle and evangelist, December 27: Gregory of Nyssa (ca. 330–ca. 395) notes this as a day for James and John; by the Leonine Sacramentary in the 600s this day is dedicated only to John the apostle and evangelist. John is the only one of the Twelve believed to have died a natural death, so the color is white. The symbol of John's Gospel is the eagle. Scriptures are Exod. 33:18-23; Ps. 92:1-4, 11-14; 1 John 1:1-9; John 21:9b-24. Hymns and songs include: Shout to the Lord (Zschech); When at this table (Murray); Come, pure hearts, in joyful measure (Latin, twelfth century); Praise God for John, evangelist (Janzow).

Feast of the Holy Innocents, December 28: The Feast of the Holy Innocents first appeared in 505 in the calendar for the city of Carthage in North Africa (Adolf Adam, *The Liturgical Year* [New York: Pueblo, 1981], 143), and its scriptures are Jer. 31:15-17; Ps. 124; Rev. 21:1-7; Matt. 2:13-18. The traditional carol for this event: Lullay, la lu, thou little tiny child (trad. medieval carol). For other resources, see Year A, the Sunday after Christmas, chapter 3.

The Holy Name of Jesus Christ, New Year's Day, January 1: Scriptures for this day are Num. 6:22-27; Ps. 8; Gal. 4:4-7; Luke 2:15-21. Names and adjectives for God, particularly appropriate to this day are Alpha and Omega; Eternal God; God of Fresh Beginnings; God of the Ages; God, who wears a human name; God, whose name endures to all generations; and Majestic Name.

Hymns, Songs, and Spirituals

Blessing from Numbers 6, settings by Lutkin, Winter, and Strathdee

A mother lined a basket (Keithahn); The virgin Mary had a baby boy (trad. West Indian); Now greet the swiftly changing year (Slovak); Jesus! Name of wondrous love! (How)

Doxologies

Jesus, the very thought of thee, often attributed to Bernard of Clairvaux (ca. 1090–1153), contains the following verse. Sing it to AMAZING GRACE, CHRISTMAS (While shepherds watched their flocks by night), or ANTIOCH, (Joy to the world, inserting the lines in parentheses).

Nor voice can sing, nor heart can frame,

nor can the memory find,

a sweeter sound than your blest name,

Savior of humankind.

(Jesus of Bethlehem,

God's Light to all the world,

to all the world.)

Epiphany: Burn a candle or stick of frankincense, symbolizing the gift brought by the Magi to honor the God in the child Jesus.

Epiphany Vigil: There is a strong tradition in the Orthodox Church of a Vigil service for the Feast of the **Theophany,** as Epiphany is known there. Because of the intersection of the birth of Jesus and his baptism on this day in that tradition, the Vigil includes readings about water and baptism from throughout the scriptures—creation, the taking of the baby Moses from the river, passing through the Red Sea, water from the rock in the wilderness, crossing the Jordan, streams in the desert, John the Baptist, Jesus' baptism, the rivers of Revelation. A full list may be found in *A Christmas Sourcebook,* 129–130.

Protestants might combine these readings with the pattern of the Easter Vigil adapted for Epiphany: the Light that enters is the incarnational symbol of Jesus Christ entering into human time as the Light of the World, then the Word as noted above, followed by baptism and communion.

Ordinary Time

During the early twentieth century, there was a movement to create a liturgical season during Ordinary Time after Pentecost to reflect the Social Gospel, called **Kingdomtide,** which would focus on *missio Dei* and circumstances of human living. The Federal Council of Churches promoted the season, but eventually it was only retained by the Methodists and

American Baptists (see James F. White, *A Brief History of Christian Worship* [Nashville: Abingdon, 1993], 163; Fred Winslow Adams, *The Christian Year,* 2nd ed. [New York: Federal Council of Churches, 1940], 4; John E. Skoglund and Nancy E. Hall, *A Manual of Worship,* new edition [Valley Forge, Pa.: Judson, 1993], 95). Laurence Hull Stookey mentions that the 1945 Methodist *Book of Worship* designated the last Sunday of August as the "Festival of Christ the King" to inaugurate the season of Kingdomtide, which went from this Sunday to the beginning of Advent; subsequent Methodist books of worship did not retain this inaugural Sunday for Kingdomtide (Stookey, *Calendar: Christ's Time for the Church* [Nashville: Abingdon, 1996], 182n. 4).

Early in the twenty-first century, the Uniting Church in Australia suggested that six weeks of Ordinary Time, four in September and the first two in October, might be used to focus on creation, to confess our misuse of it and to commit to partner with God in its healing. This **Season of Creation** has also been promoted in an article in *Worship Arts* by Daniel Benedict of The United Methodist Church. There is an extensive website, Season of Creation, developed for this proposed season, with themes for each week: http://www.seasonofcreation.com/. With current concerns about global warming and other environmental issues, this season may be helpful in some congregations; it does overlook World Communion Sunday but otherwise it fits easily into the current Christian year.

James F. White suggests that **remembering the saints** of the church is becoming an option for Protestant Christians ("Forgetting and Remembering the Saints," in *Between Memory and Hope* [BMH] [Collegeville, Minn.: Liturgical Press, 2000], 401–414). James Baldovin, S.J., claims that this is because of the human need for "tangible reminders that God's power has been at work in human beings" ("The Liturgical Year: Calendar for a Just Community," in *BMH,* 436). Baldovin then suggests some unofficial contemporary saints who might be incorporated into preaching and prayers on their memorial days (*BMH*, 442–443). These and several others have been included in the list below.

Churches looking to enrich their worship with the traditions of the church might add appropriate scriptures and songs, and a brief prayer related to the gifts of the Christian named.

Sanctoral Calendar

Nov. 30, Andrew the apostle

Dec. 2, the Four Women Martyrs of El Salvador: Maura Clark, Jean Donovan, Ita Ford, and Dorothy Kazel

Dec. 21, Thomas the apostle

Dec. 26, Stephen, first martyr

Dec. 27, John the apostle and evangelist

Dec. 28, Feast of the Holy Innocents

Jan. 1, Mary, the Mother of God; Holy Name of Jesus

3rd Monday of January, Martin Luther King, Jr.

Jan. 25, the conversion of Paul

Feb. 2, the presentation of Christ in the Temple

Feb. 24, Mathias the apostle

March 10, Harriet Tubman

March 12, Rutilio Grande, Salvadoran priest

March 24, Archbishop Oscar Romero

March 25, Annunciation to Mary

April 9, Dietrich Bonhoeffer

April 25, Mark the evangelist

May 1, Philip and James, apostles

May 8, Julian of Norwich

June 11, Barnabas the apostle

June 24, John the Baptist

June 29, Peter the apostle

July 22, Mary Magdalene, first witness to the resurrection

Aug. 11, Clare of Assisi

Aug. 24, Bartholomew the apostle

Sept. 14, Holy Cross

Sept. 17, Hildegard of Bingen

Sept. 18, Dag Hammarskjöld

Sept. 21, Matthew, apostle and evangelist

Sept. 29, Michael and all angels

Oct. 4, Francis of Assisi

Oct. 18, Luke the evangelist

Oct. 28, Simon and Jude, apostles

Nov. 1, All Saints' Day

Nov. 16, the Jesuit martyrs of El Salvador and their companions

Nov. 26, Sojourner Truth

Nov. 29, Dorothy Day

Within the Wesleyan movement, there is a tradition of using the **Covenant Service,** developed by John Wesley from the seventeenth-century Puritans and eighteenth-century Moravians, on New Year's Eve or the First Sunday of the New Year. Given the current popularity and ecumenism of reaffirmation/renewal of baptism on Baptism of Jesus Christ Sunday so soon after the New Year, rather than using the Wesley Covenant Renewal Service then, consider using it on Aldersgate Sunday (closest to May 24, as John Wesley experienced his "heart strangely warmed" on that date in 1738) or during Ordinary Time in the summer. For more information, see books of worship from the Wesleyan tradition, including *Methodist Worship Book* (Peterborough, Great Britain: Methodist Publishing, 1999).

Many congregations join with the Pontifical Council for Promoting

Christian Unity (Roman Catholic) and the World Council of Churches (Protestant and Orthodox) in celebrating the **Week of Prayer for Christian Unity, January 18–25**. Churches join across denominations to hold services together on an evening or include concerns for Christian unity in their prayers for that Sunday. Resources for each year can be found on the World Council of Churches' website, http://www.oikoumene.org/en/pro grammes/unity-mission-evangelism-and-spirituality/spirituality-and-worship/week-of-prayer-for-christian-unity.html.

Feb. 2, Presentation of Christ in the Temple: This day celebrates the events of Luke 2:22-38 as Mary and Joseph presented Jesus in the Temple and met Simeon and Anna forty days after Jesus' birth. It links the infant Jesus with the prophecies of the Jewish people for a Messiah. In the Eastern Orthodox Church, the meeting of Mary, Joseph, Jesus, Simeon, and Anna is a sign of the new community in Christ (*The New Westminster Dictionary of Liturgy and Worship* (2005), s.v. "Candlemas." Kenneth W. Stevenson). This day takes the name **Candlemas** from the blessing of candles; parishioners would bring candles for the church along with ones they would take home again, and all would be blessed on this day and processed around the church while Simeon's Nunc Dimittis was sung. As one writer says, "Today the light of Christmas is placed in our very arms" (Peter Mazar, *Keeping Advent and Christmastime* [Chicago: Liturgy Training Publications, 1996], 48). For more information see Senn, *The People's Work*, 154–155; and Eamon Duffy, *The Stripping of the Altars: Traditional Religion in England 1400–1580* (New Haven: Yale University Press, 1992), 15–18.

Annunciation, March 25: This day celebrates the visitation of the angel Gabriel to Mary to announce God's intention for her to bear the Son of the Most High. For many denominations Mary's willingness to do as God asked has become the model for all Christians' responses to God.

Acts 6:5-15, the story of **Stephen and the first deacons,** is not in the *RCL*; use it in a service to commission deacons, to explain and honor their work. The song Within the day-to-day (Thornburg) was written for deacons, who bridge the church and world. Other appropriate hymns and songs include Jesu, Jesu, fill us with your love (Colvin); As a fire is meant for burning (Duck); The Spirit sends us forth to serve (Dufner).

St. Francis Day, October 4, is often celebrated with a blessing of parishioners' pets and can be a good community outreach as it can be held on the church lawn.

Reformation Sunday: Some Protestant churches, particularly Lutherans and Presbyterians, have observed Reformation Sunday on the last Sunday of October or October 31, honoring the day in 1517 when Martin Luther may have posted his "95 Theses" on the church door in Wittenberg, Germany. This celebration is less common since the time of the Roman Calendar in 1969 and the *RCL*, as this bumps into All Saints, observances. The United Methodist *Book of Worship* suggests using prayers for the church as well as Luther's hymn, A mighty fortress is our God.

All Saints: Consider using the Wisdom of Solomon 3:1-9 appointed for this day in some lectionaries, Year B. Hymns and spirituals that fit this scripture: O what their joy and their glory must be (Abelard); My Lord, what a morning (spiritual).

During Ordinary Time in Months of June through November

The *RCL* includes alternative Hebrew Scriptures and Psalms for each Sunday (for songs for the Epistle and Gospel, which remain the same, see the corresponding dates in chapter 4).

Year A

• May 29–June 4, if after Trinity Sunday: Deut. 11:18-21, 26-28; Ps. 31:1-5, 19-24; Saranam, saranam (trad. Pakistani); On eagle's wings (Joncas)

• June 5–11, if after Trinity Sunday: Hos. 5:15–6:6; Ps. 50:7-15; Kyrie, eleison (Taizé); What does the Lord require of you? (Strathdee)

• June 12–18, if after Trinity Sunday: Exod. 19:2-8a; Ps. 100; Jubilate Deo (Taizé); Rejoice in God, all earthly lands (Duck)

• June 19–25, if after Trinity Sunday: Jer. 20:7-13; Ps. 69:7-10, (11-15), 16-18; O God, your Word, a raging fire (Bringle); When we are tested and wrestle alone (Duck)

• June 26–July 2: Jer. 28:5-9; Ps. 89:1-4, 15-18; Great is thy/your faithfulness (Chisholm); Amen, amen, it shall be so (Bell)

• July 3–9: Zech. 9:9-12; Ps. 145:8-14; Rejoice in the Lord, alway (anon.); Come, thou fount of every blessing (Robinson)

• July 10–16: Isa. 55:10-13; Ps. 65:(1-8), 9-13; Light dawns on a weary world (Bringle); You shall go out with joy (Ruben)

• July 17–23: Isa. 44:6-8; Ps. 86:11-17; Guide me, O thou great Jehovah (Williams); Sing praise to God who reigns above (Schütz)

• July 24–30: 1 Kgs. 3:5-12; Ps. 119:129-136; Come and seek the ways of wisdom (Duck); Order my steps in your Word (Burleigh)

• July 31–Aug. 6: Isa. 55:1-5; Ps. 145:8-9, 14-21; You who are thirsty (Ross); There's a wideness in God's mercy (Faber)

• Aug. 7–13: 1 Kgs. 19:9-18; Ps. 85:8-13; God grant us greening (Bringle); The kingdom of God is justice and peace (Taizé)

• Aug. 14–20: Isa. 56:1, 6-8; Ps. 67; Gather us in (Haugen); The Lord bless you and keep you (Strathdee)

• Aug. 21–27: Isa. 51:1-6; Ps. 138; We sing to you, O God (Grindal); Kyrie, eleison (Taizé)

• Aug. 28–Sept. 3: Jer. 15:15-21; Ps. 26:1-8; When we are tested and wrestle alone (Duck); Seek the Lord who now is present (Pratt Green)

• Sept. 4–10: Ezek. 33:7-11; Ps. 119:33-40; Come back quickly to the Lord (Chun); Seek the Lord who now is present (Pratt Green)

• Sept. 11–17: Gen. 50:15-21; Ps. 103:(1-7), 8-13; Bless the Lord, O my soul (Crouch); Forgive our sins as we forgive (Herklots)

• Sept. 18–24: Jonah 3:10–4:11; Ps. 145:1-8; Your love, O God (Frostenson); Bless the Lord (Taizé)

• Sept. 25–Oct. 1: Ezek. 18:1-4, 25-32; Ps. 25:1-9; Seek the Lord who now is present (Pratt Green); I will trust in the Lord (spiritual)

• Oct. 2–8: Isa. 5:1-7; Ps. 80:7-15; Creator of the earth and skies (Hughes); Response for use throughout the service (Ps. 80:7)

• Oct. 9–15: Isa. 25:1-9; Ps. 23; We sing to you, O God (Grindal); Shepherd me, O God (Haugen)

• Oct. 16–22: Isa. 45:1-7; Ps. 96:1-9, (10-13); Praise to the Lord (Klusmeier); We sing of your glory/Tuya es la gloria (trad.)

• Oct. 23–29: Lev. 19:1-2, 15-18; Ps. 1; Tell us, Rabbi, is it lawful (Bringle); How firm a foundation (anon.)

• Oct. 30–Nov. 5, if All Saints not observed on this day: Micah 3:5-12, Ps. 43; How shall they hear the word of God (Perry); As pants the deer (Duck)

• Nov. 6–12: Amos 5:18-24; Ps. 70; Let justice roll like flowing streams (Aldredge-Clanton); O Lord, hear my prayer (Taizé)

• Nov. 13–19: Zeph. 1:7, 12-18; Ps. 90:1-8, (9-11), 12; My Lord, what a morning (spiritual); O God, our help in ages past (Watts)

Year B

• May 29–June 4, if after Trinity Sunday: Deut. 5:12-15; Ps. 81:1-10; Come Sunday (Ellington); Praise ye the Lord (Cleveland)

• June 5–11, if after Trinity Sunday: Gen. 3:8-15; Ps. 130; Come back quickly to the Lord (Chun); Out of the depths (Duck)

• June 12–18, if after Trinity Sunday: Ezek. 17:22-24; Ps. 92:1-4, 12-15; Let all things now living (Davis); Praise the Lord with the sound of trumpet (Sleeth)

• June 19–25, if after Trinity Sunday: Job 38:1-11; Ps. 107:1-3, 23-32; From the whirlwind (Bringle); In the Lord I'll be ever thankful (Taizé)

• June 26–July 2: Lam. 3:23-33; Ps. 30: Great is your faithfulness (Chisholm); Tuya es la gloria/We sing of your glory (trad.)

• July 3–9: Ezek. 2:1-5; Ps. 123; Stand, O stand firm (trad. Cameroonian); Kyrie, eleison (Taizé)

• July 10–16: Amos 7:7-15; Ps. 85:8-13: God has spoken by the prophets (Briggs); Santo/Holy (Cuéllar); La palabra del Dios es recta (García)

• July 17–23: Jer. 23:1-6; Ps. 23; God the Spirit, Guide and Guardian (Daw); My shepherd is the Lord (Gelineau)

• July 24–30: 2 Kgs. 4:42-44; Ps. 145:10-18; Eat this bread (Taizé); Thank you, Lord (trad.); Come, all you people (Gondo)

• July 31–Aug. 6: Exod. 16:2-4, 9-15; Ps. 78:23-29; Eat this bread (Taizé); O food to pilgrims given (trans. Athelstan and Riley)

• Aug. 7–13: 1 Kgs. 19:4-8; Ps. 34:1-8; O food to pilgrims given (trans. Athelstan and Riley); Bless the Lord, O my soul (Crouch)

• Aug. 14–20: Prov. 9:1-6; Ps. 34:9-14; Wisdom is calling (Joncas); Praise the Source of faith and learning (Troeger)

• Aug. 21–27: Josh. 24:1-2a, 14-18; Ps. 34:15-22; Love the Lord your God (Strathdee); Now praise the hidden God of love (Pratt Green)

• Aug. 28–Sept. 3: Deut. 4:1-2, 6-9; Ps. 15; Love the Lord your God (Strathdee); We are called (Haas)

• Sept. 4–10: Isa. 35:4-7a; Ps. 146; Marching to Zion (Watts and Lowry); O for a thousand tongues to sing (Wesley)

• Sept. 11–17: Isa. 50:4-9a; Ps. 116:1-9; If thou but suffer God to guide thee (Neumark); O God, beyond all praising (Perry)

• Sept. 18–24: Jer. 11:18-20; Ps. 54; Surely, it is God who saves me (White); Praise to the Lord (Klusmeier)

• Sept. 25–Oct. 1: Num. 11:4-6, 10-16, 24-29; Ps. 19:7-14; Let my people seek their freedom (O'Driscoll); Wake every breath and string (Bringle)

• Oct. 2–8: Gen. 2:18-24; Ps. 8; Womb of life, and Source of being (Duck); O Lord, our Lord, how majestic is your name (Smith)

• Oct. 9–15: Amos 5:6-7, 10-15; Ps. 90:12-17; Seek the Lord, who now is present (Pratt Green); Forgive us, Lord (Lockward)

• Oct. 16–22: Isa. 53:4-12; Ps. 91:9-16; Rejected and despised (Bringle); On eagle's wings (Joncas)

• Oct. 23–29: Jer. 31:7-9; Ps. 126; North, south, and west and east (Duck); refrain: Bringing in the sheaves (Shaw)

• Oct. 30–Nov. 5: Deut. 6:1-9; Ps. 119:1-8; If all you want, Lord, is my heart (Troeger); North, south, and west and east (Duck)

• Nov. 6–12: 1 Kgs. 17:8-16; Ps. 146; I will trust in the Lord (spiritual); Praise ye the Lord (Cleveland)

• Nov. 13–19: Dan. 12:1-3; Ps. 16; My Lord, what a morning (spiritual); Bless the Lord, my soul (Taizé)

Year C

• May 29–June 4, if after Trinity Sunday: 1 Kgs. 8:22-23, 41-43; Ps. 96:1-9; Immortal, invisible, God only wise (Smith); We sing of your glory/Tuya es la gloria (trad.)

• June 5–11, if after Trinity Sunday: 1 Kgs. 17:17-24; Ps. 30; I will trust in the Lord (spiritual); Held in the shelter of God's wing (Bringle)

• June 12–18, if after Trinity Sunday: 2 Sam. 11:26–12:10, 13-15; Ps. 32; Depth of mercy (Wesley); It is well with my soul (Spafford)

• June 19–25, if after Trinity Sunday: Isa. 65:1-9; Ps. 22:19-28; God has spoken by the prophets (Briggs); Come back quickly to the Lord (Chun)

• June 26–July 2: 1 Kgs. 19:15-16, 19-21; Ps. 16; How shall they hear the word of God (Perry); Bless the Lord (Taizé)

• July 3–9: Isa. 66:10-14; Ps. 66:1-9; Bring many names (Wren); Praise to the Lord, the almighty (Neander)

• July 10–16: Deut. 30:9-14; Ps. 25:1-10; Thy word is a lamp unto my feet (Grant); Lead me, Lord/God (Wesley)

• July 17–23: Gen. 18:1-10a; Ps. 15; Come in from the cold, my friend (Damon); We are called (Haas)

• July 24–30: Gen. 18:20-32; Ps. 138; Forgive us, Lord (Lockward); Thank you, Lord (trad.)

• July 31–Aug. 6: Eccl. 1:2, 12-14; 2:18-23; Ps. 49:1-12; Seek ye first (Lafferty); Leave it there (Tindley)

• Aug. 7–13: Gen. 15:1-6; Ps. 33:12-22; I will trust in the Lord (spiritual); Come, all who long for peace on earth (Duck)

• Aug. 14–20: Jer. 23:23-29; Ps. 82; Come, divine Interpreter (Wesley); Seek the Lord who now is present (Pratt Green)

• Aug. 21–27: Isa. 58:9b-14; Ps. 103:1-8; We are called (Haas); Bless the Lord, O my soul (Crouch)

• Aug. 28–Sept. 3: Prov. 25:6-7; Ps. 112; Jesu, Jesu, fill us with your love (Colvin); We are called (Haas)

• Sept. 4–10: Deut. 30:15-20; Ps. 1; Dear Lord, lead me day by day (Asuncion); Thy Word is a lamp unto my feet (Grant)

• Sept. 11–17: Exod. 32:7-14; Ps. 51:1-10; Let my people seek their freedom (O'Driscoll); Give me a clean heart (Douroux)

• Sept. 18–24: Amos 8:4-7; Ps. 113; When the church of Jesus shuts its outer door (Pratt Green); Praise to the Lord (Klusmeier)

• Sept. 25–Oct. 1: Amos 6:1a, 4-7; Ps. 146; When the church of Jesus shuts its outer door (Pratt Green); Blessed be the God of Israel (Perry)

• Oct. 2–8: Hab. 1:1-4; 2:1-4; Ps. 37:1-9; Be thou my vision (ancient Irish); I will trust in the Lord (spiritual)

• Oct. 9–15: 2 Kgs. 5:1-3, 7-15c; Ps. 111; The God of Abraham praise (ben Judah); Heal us, Emmanuel, hear our prayer (verses 1, 2, 5) (Cowper)

• Oct. 16–22: Gen. 32:22-31; Ps. 121; Come, O thou Traveler unknown (Wesley); Dios está aquí/God is here today (trad. Mexican)

• Oct. 23–29: Jer. 14:7-10, 19-22; Ps. 84:1-7; Forgive us, Lord/Perdón, Dios (Lockward); How lovely, Lord (Duba)

• Oct. 30–Nov. 5: Isa. 1:10-18; Ps. 32:1-7; What does the Lord require of you? (Strathdee); You are my hiding place (Ledner)

• Nov. 6–12: Job 19:23-27a; Ps. 17:1-9; Held in the shelter of God's wing (Bringle); I know that my Redeemer lives (from *Messiah*, Handel)

• Nov. 13–19: Mal. 4:1-2a; Ps. 98; Hark! The herald angels sing (verse 3, Wesley); To God compose a song of joy (Duck)

CPSIA information can be obtained at www.ICGtesting.com
Printed in the USA
LVOW11s2048280316

481141LV00004B/52/P